Great
Auto Makers
and Their Cars

GREAT
AUTO MAKERS
AND THEIR CARS

Robert Italia

illustrated with photographs

The Oliver Press, Inc.,
Minneapolis

The Oliver Press
Josiah King House
2709 Lyndale Avenue South
Minneapolis, MN 55408

Library of Congress Cataloging-in-Publication Data

Italia, Robert, 1955-
Great auto makers and their cars / Robert Italia.
p.   cm. — (Profiles)
Includes bibliographical references and index.
    Summary: Introduces some of the men whose ideas and innovations shaped the development of modern automobiles, including Karl Benz, Ferdinand Porsche, William Lyons, and Henry Ford.
ISBN 1-881508-08-0 : $14.95
1. Automobile engineers—Biography—Juvenile literature.
[1. Automobile Engineers. 2. Automobiles—History.] I. Title.
II. Series: Profiles (Minneapolis, Minn.)
TL139. I82 1993
629.2'2'092'2—dc20
[B]   92-43464
                                                                                    CIP
                                                                                     AC

ISBN 1-881508-08-0
Profiles VIII
Printed in the United States of America

99 98 97 96 95 94 93   8 7 6 5 4 3 2 1

Contents

Introduction 7

Chapter 1   Karl Benz and Mercedes 11
Chapter 2   Henry Ford...29
Chapter 3   The Dodge Brothers 49
Chapter 4   Ferdinand Porsche 61
Chapter 5   William Lyons and Jaguar 83
Chapter 6   Alfred Sloan and General Motors...........99
Chapter 7   Enzo Ferrari 113
Chapter 8   Soichiro Honda 131
Chapter 9   Ferruccio Lamborghini.........................143

Bibliography 154
Index 155

Introduction

*P*erhaps no invention in the history of humankind has transformed the face of the earth more than the automobile. The auto allows you to travel great distances and see things you might not normally get to see. The auto takes you to school or work. It allows you to bring food and clothing to your home. It entertains and fascinates you with its speed, power, and sleek design. It keeps you safe and dry when you venture out into stormy weather. Functioning day to day without this mechanical wonder would be extremely difficult.

You owe a lot to the people who developed the automobile. But do you know the names behind the gleaming chrome, sparkling glass, and painted molded panels that make up your favorite car? Who were these people? What special talents did they have? And what attracted them to the automobile?

Contrary to what many think, Henry Ford did not

invent the automobile. That distinction went to Karl Benz, the father of the modern motor car. What Henry Ford did was make the automobile affordable to the working people of the world. Ferdinand Porsche adopted this concept when he designed the world-famous Volkswagen for Germany's leader Adolf Hitler.

All the designers in this book had one important thing in common: they loved the automobile. And their love often began at an early age—despite discouragement from their family.

Ferruccio Lamborghini was the son of an Italian farmer. His father wanted him to till the soil. But young Lamborghini had other ideas. The farm equipment and how it worked fascinated him. This fascination led Lamborghini to an engineering career. Eventually he designed some of the most famous *gran turismo* cars in the world.

Ferdinand Porsche was the son of a German tinsmith. His father wanted him to carry on the family business. But Porsche was more interested in conducting electrical experiments in his father's house. Finally, Porsche's parents sent him to a nearby technical school. Eventually he established himself as one of the most productive and influential automotive designers in history.

The father of William Lyons groomed him to take over the family's piano business. But motorcycles and motorcars interested young William. Lyons went on to design one of the most recognized sports cars in the history of automobile manufacturing—the Jaguar.

The automobile's power fascinated all these innovative designers. They saw its potential to improve people's lives. And they continually toyed with their designs, looking for newer and better ways to make their cars run farther and faster. Their work wasn't glamorous. Often a designer rolled up his sleeves, grabbed a wrench, and crawled under the oily car to fix his newly created machine. Sometimes a designer spent years drawing up plans for a new car—only to see these blueprints shelved because of lack of money. Other times, designers fell victim to business squabbles and jealousies. Some even fell victim to world politics and war. Yet they persevered.

Many people think the place for old cars and old designs is in museums. But innovations born decades ago still influence today's auto designs. Ford used the assembly line to put the world on wheels. Porsche employed front-wheel drive and air-cooled, V-shaped engines. Most of the designers in this book were pioneers. Their ingenuity and foresight made the automobile what it is today.

So the next time you hop into a car, take a closer look at its design. Think about the decades of planning that went into its construction. Perhaps you'll see some of the handiwork of these innovative auto makers.

The name of automotive pioneer Karl Benz lives on today in one of the world's most prestigious cars, the Mercedes-Benz.

1

Karl Benz and Mercedes

*A*utomotive historians consider Karl Benz and Gottlieb Daimler the founding fathers of the automobile. Yet, although they lived and worked only 60 miles apart and their auto companies eventually merged, they never met.

Karl Benz was born in Pfaffenrot, Germany, in 1844. When Benz was two years old, his father died in a train accident. Benz's mother had to work hard so Benz could go to school. After he graduated, he got a job at a nearby locomotive factory, which eventually promoted him to draftsman. There he learned to design engines and bridges.

Benz left his job to start his own machine shop in Mannheim, Germany. At first, Benz struggled, for he was an engineer, not a businessman. In 1882, Benz took on partners to help him with his business, but he did not get along with them and broke away to form another company in October 1883. He called it Benz & Company.

Benz decided to build an engine that would burn gasoline. Gasoline was new at the time, but Benz felt it was the fuel of the future. His new gasoline-powered engine sold well.

In the autumn of 1885, Benz decided to put his gasoline-powered engine on a carriage. After some major adjustments, Benz tested his three-wheeled motor-driven carriage for the first time. The engine had one cylinder. And the motor car had a top speed of 10 MPH. Benz's motor car had problems at first, and he wasn't sure if it would ever replace horse-drawn carriages. But in 1886, Benz had the foresight to patent his motor car.

By August 1888, Benz experienced financial problems again. He doubted that his motor car would ever become a success. To prove him wrong, Benz's wife, Berta, and their two oldest sons took the car on a trip. They traveled 60 miles from Mannheim to Pforzheim. Along the way, they had to push the car up hills and buy gasoline at pharmacy stores. But just after dark, they finally reached their destination.

The successful trip caused quite a stir. Until that time, the public considered the motor car a toy.

The first car in history was a three-wheeled carriage created by Karl Benz.

Suddenly people began to see it as a dependable and useful means of transportation. More importantly, demand for Benz's motor car grew, and his business prospered.

Benz continued to improve his motor car design. In 1893, he built his first four-wheel car: the Victoria. It had a one-cylinder engine and a top speed of 21 MPH. In July 1894, an Austrian businessman drove a Benz Victoria from Reichenberg, Bohemia, through Germany and on to Reims, France. Then he made the return trip to Reichenberg. The three-country, 1,000-mile trip proved that Benz's automobiles were the best in the world.

That same month, the very first automobile race was held in France. The 78-mile race started in Paris and ended in Rouen. The race was open to any carriage without a horse and the size of the engine or the car did not matter.

However, Karl Benz did not want his automobiles in the race. Benz built high-quality cars for the wealthy in Europe. He considered racing undignified and dangerous. But Emile Roger, Benz's French car distributor, ignored his request and entered a Benz in the race. The car proved its reliability by finishing the race. However, it finished last to all other gasoline-powered automobiles—including the winning vehicle, powered by a Daimler engine.

In 1895, Roger entered a Benz Phaeton in the 732-mile Paris-Bordeaux-Paris race. Out of 22 cars, only 9 completed the race. The Phaeton finished seventh. The winning car took 90 hours to complete the course. It, too, was powered by a Daimler engine, built by Gottlieb Daimler.

The two races enhanced Benz's reputation for quality and durability. But the speed and power of the Daimler engines intrigued auto enthusiasts. Clearly, Gottlieb Daimler was Karl Benz's major competitor.

Gottlieb Daimler was born in 1834 in Schorndorf, Germany. Trained as an engineer, Daimler worked in

The Benz Phaeton chugs along in the 1895 Paris-Bordeaux-Paris race.

several factories before retiring in December 1881. In his private greenhouse, working with protégé Wilhelm Maybach, Daimler began developing compact, fast-running engines.

In 1883, Daimler built and patented a gasoline-powered engine. He took this idea one step further in 1885, when he designed and patented a water-cooled engine. Since internal combustion engines create a lot of heat, they require a cooling system to keep temperatures down. In Daimler's system, cool water circulated around the engine block and protected the engine from overheating. This idea is still used on most of today's automobiles. Now he was ready to test his engines on a vehicle.

Gottlieb Daimler's early work on the internal combustion engine paved the way for future improvements in automobile operation.

Daimler's first motorized vehicle was not a car but a bicycle. Thus, Daimler invented the motorcycle. His second motorized vehicle was a boat—Daimler had invented the power boat.

Daimler built and patented his first automobile in the autumn of 1886. It had four wheels, a one-cylinder engine, and a top speed of 10 MPH. While Karl Benz spent his time designing and building the best cars, Daimler formed the Daimler company in Stuttgart and

Daimler's 1886 car

concentrated on building the best engines. A better businessman than Benz, Daimler put his powerful engines in trucks, fire engines, boats, and trolley cars. And he expanded his company to foreign cities, including Paris, New York, and London.

Still, Benz's reputation for quality remained strong. By 1899, Benz & Company—now called Benz & Cie— had become the world's largest car manufacturer. That same year, Emil Jellinek, a wealthy Austrian business- man and diplomat, saw a Daimler Phoenix win a race in Nice, France. The car so impressed him that he approached Daimler with a business proposition. Jellinek would purchase 36 cars if Daimler built a new, more powerful model. Jellinek suggested that the new model be called Mercedes, named after Jellinek's daughter. Daimler agreed to the business deal. But he never saw the Mercedes completed, for he died in 1900.

Daimler Motoren Gesellschaft (DMG)—Daimler's company—introduced the first Mercedes in 1901. The world had never seen anything like it. The new Mercedes sat lower to the ground than other vehicles. Its wheels were set wider apart for better cornering. The car had four speeds, including reverse, and could reach a top speed of 47 MPH. Even more, the

The first car to carry the name Mercedes, in 1901, to honor the daughter of Daimler's partner, Emil Jellinek

Mercedes engine had four cylinders. It is considered the first modern car.

That same year, a Mercedes set a world speed record of 49.4 MPH on a one-mile drive at Nice. By 1902, the Mercedes was the talk of the auto world and dominated new car sales.

Over the next few years, Mercedes continued to set the automotive world on end with its high performance. In 1904, a Mercedes was clocked at an amazing 97.2 MPH over a one-kilometer stretch. (1.6 km = 1 mile.) The following year, a Mercedes with two 60-horsepower engines set another world record of 109.6 MPH at a Daytona Beach, Florida, racetrack.

This American Mercedes model was produced in the United States between 1905 and 1907.

American daredevil Barney Oldfield raced the Blitzen Benz at many county fair dirt tracks.

With all the attention Mercedes was receiving because of its racing success, Karl Benz reluctantly decided to construct race cars of his own. In 1908, Benz built the Grand Prix Benz for the French Grand Prix. The race turned out to be a showdown between Benz and Mercedes. After a nip-and-tuck battle along the 477-mile course, Mercedes finished first.

In 1909, Benz introduced the *Blitzen Benz* (Lightning Benz). It had an enormous 200-horsepower engine and proved to be a formidable foe to Mercedes. In 1911, the Blitzen Benz set a world record of 141.7 MPH at Daytona Beach—a record that stood for 15 years. In 1913, Benz recorded 29 racing victories while Mercedes recorded only 13.

Between 1914 and 1918, World War I brought a halt to car production in Germany. Benz and Daimler turned their engineering talents to their country's war effort, building trucks and other military equipment. The German military also used Benz and Daimler engines in its warplanes.

After the war, Germany was in a shambles. Many years passed before its auto industry recovered. Mercedes, however, was eventually able to return to sports car production. In 1922, Mercedes developed a supercharged engine designed by Ferdinand Porsche. The supercharger force-fed fuel and air into an engine, thus making it more powerful. By 1923, Porsche had become Daimler's chief engineer.

Benz concentrated on building trucks, which Germany needed for reconstruction. In 1924, the Benz company introduced the first diesel truck. A diesel engine, named after its inventor, Rudolf Diesel, was more fuel efficient and provided more power.

In 1926, the Daimler and the Benz companies merged and became Mercedes-Benz. Benz's symbol, a laurel wreath, encircled Daimler's symbol, a three-pointed star. The new company placed the word *Mercedes* on top of the symbol and displayed the word *Benz* on the bottom. This famous symbol is still used today.

Mercedes-Benz introduced the Stuttgart in 1928. Named for the city where DMG started, it had a six-cylinder engine and a top speed of 56 MPH. After the death of Karl Benz in 1929, his company drew up plans for the Mannheim, which was named for the city where

Benz & Co. originated. Introduced in 1931, the Mannheim had a more powerful six-cylinder engine and a top speed of 75 MPH. Both the Stuttgart and the Mannheim sold well, guaranteeing the success of Mercedes-Benz.

In 1934, the German government decided to sponsor an auto racing program. In response, Mercedes-Benz built the W25. In its first year, the W25 won 16 major races. The W25 and successive models went on to dominate the racing scene of the 1930s.

In 1938, the W125, a W25 successor, raced on the Frankfurt-to-Heidelberg autobahn (highway). It reached a top speed of 271 MPH—the record for the fastest mile on a public road, which still stands today.

The world-famous symbol of Mercedes-Benz, which grew out of the merger between the Daimler and Benz companies, adorns the hood of this Mannheim.

Around the same time, Mercedes-Benz decided to construct the world's fastest automobile. It was called the T80, and Ferdinand Porsche led the project. The T80 had a 12-cylinder airplane engine and four rear wheels for maximum drive. More importantly, the T80 was incredibly aerodynamic; that is, the car had very little wind resistance. The company conducted early test runs in the autumn of 1939. The estimated top speed was 406 MPH.

But just when the T80 was ready to race, World War II began. Once again, Mercedes-Benz halted all car production and concentrated on the war effort. The military had Mercedes-Benz convert most of its trucks for military use. Daimler-Benz built engines for the German army's famous Panther and Tiger tanks and for the Messerschmitt fighter planes and bombers.

Allied bombers pounded German industry into rubble and destroyed many of the Mercedes-Benz factories. But the Mannheim factory received the least amount of damage. The company had restored the factory by the late 1940s and thus could produce the trucks and buses that Germany needed to recover from the war.

In 1948, Mercedes-Benz introduced the multipurpose Unimog, which could be used as a farm tractor or as a transporter. It could also be driven over rough terrain and had a top speed of 43 MPH. The Unimog helped Germany in rebuilding its war-torn towns and cities.

By 1950, Mercedes-Benz was building cars again— more, in fact, than at any time in its long history. The 220 and 300 were the first two models to roll out of the new factories. The company designed the 220 as a mid-class car. The 300 was a luxury car built for the international market. It became one of Mercedes-Benz's most successful models and sold well into the 1970s. The 300 also set the standard for today's S-Class Mercedes. With the 300's success, auto enthusiasts recognized Mercedes-Benz once again for high quality.

Mercedes returned to the racing scene in 1952 with the 300 SL. It had a rounded body, gull-wing doors that lifted upward, and a steering wheel that came off so the driver could get in and out more easily. As a race car, the 300 SL collected many first-place trophies, including victories at Le Mans, the German Grand Prix, and the Carrera Panamericana in Mexico.

Mercedes-Benz's involvement in racing ended suddenly and tragically in 1955. During the 24-hour race at Le Mans, a 300 SL tangled with an Austin-Healy near the pit area. The crash caused minor damage to the car, but spectators were crowded in great numbers along the pit area. The SL careened out of control and plowed into the spectators, killing over 80 people. It was one of the worst auto racing disasters ever. Out of respect for the victims, Mercedes pulled its cars out of the race while leading.

Mercedes-Benz finished the 1955 racing season but

The Mercedes-Benz 300 SL with open gull-wing doors

then withdrew from organized racing altogether until 1987. With its 4,400-plus victories, no other auto maker has won more races than Mercedes-Benz.

In 1954, Mercedes-Benz introduced the 300 SL coupe road car in New York. The two-door coupe had a six-cylinder engine and a top speed of 155 MPH. The 300 SL created such a sensation that wealthy people all over the world waited in line to buy it. However, because the gull-wing doors were difficult to use, the company built only 1,400 coupes, the last rolling out of the factory in 1957. Still, auto experts considered the 300 SL coupe the most exciting sports car of the decade. Today it remains a highly prized collector's car.

The 300 SL convertible with conventional doors replaced the coupe. It sold well into the early 1960s.

One of the most popular Mercedes-Benz luxury cars, the 450 SL convertible

Then in 1963, Mercedes-Benz introduced the 230 SL. Its most unusual feature was its "pagoda roof." It was a detachable hardtop. Once the owner removed the hardtop, the 230 SL became a traditional convertible. This roof has become the trademark of the SL and is found on today's models.

Through the 1970s and 1980s, Mercedes-Benz concentrated on expanding its line of luxury cars—including a line of limousines. Many of the 300s were custom-built to a customer's specifications. Heads of state and celebrities from around the world were seen driving their customized Mercedes-Benz cars.

When you look at the history of Mercedes-Benz, you see the history of the automobile. Karl Benz, Gottlieb Daimler, and the company they created have been involved in every significant development of the auto industry. Mercedes-Benz remains an innovator of automobile design and a symbol of engineering excellence.

Today, Mercedes-Benz offers 54 models, ranging from the compact 190, to the mid-sized 300s, to the big S-Class Mercedes—including the top-of-the-line 600 SEC. No other cars in the world hold their resale value better, for Mercedes-Benz is regarded as the world's most durable car—something that Karl Benz would be proud of.

Young Henry Ford. In building the Ford Motor Company, Henry became a giant of American industry—and one of the world's wealthiest men.

2

Henry Ford

*H*enry Ford did not design exotic sports cars. He gave the world the "Tin Lizzie"—the famous Model T. It was the first affordable car made for the average American—and it helped transform the face of the nation.

Henry Ford was born on July 30, 1863. He spent his early years working his on family's farm in Dearborn, Michigan. But young Henry found farm work boring and he much preferred tinkering in the farm's blacksmith shop. Ford had a natural talent for mathematics. This talent helped him design and build some machines of his own. He was certain that one day machines would take the place of horse-drawn wagons and plows.

When Ford was 17 years old, he left the family farm to work in Detroit. He found a job as an apprentice at the Flower Machine Shop. The shop made large brass and iron parts such as valves and fire hydrants. But Ford quickly grew tired of the slow working pace at Flower. After only nine months, he left. "I wanted to learn more about different things," he said.

Next, Ford became an apprentice at Detroit Drydock Company, a shipbuilding business that also built ship engines. Ford went to work in the engine shop. There he became familiar with steam engines.

By 1882, Ford had become a certified machinist. Westinghouse Company hired him to travel around Michigan to set up and repair steam engines in southern Michigan. All the while, Ford kept thinking of a better way to build a lighter, more powerful engine.

In 1888, Ford married Clara Bryant. Ford and Bryant settled down on a 40-acre farm given to him by his father, William. Ford made his living cutting and selling the timber on his property. He also repaired machinery for his neighbors. During his spare time, he tinkered in his workshop, trying to build that lightweight engine he was convinced was his future.

By 1891, Ford had worked out a design for a small internal-combustion engine, powered by gasoline. The Fords packed their belongings and moved from their farm to Detroit where Ford could perfect his design.

In Detroit, Ford got a job as chief engineer for

Clara Bryant Ford, the wife, mother, and grandmother of the men who ran the Ford Motor Company

Edison Illuminating Company. He kept the generators running that supplied electricity to Edison's customers. In his spare time, Ford worked on his gasoline engine. By December 1893, Ford had constructed his first one.

In June, Ford mounted his engine on a four-wheel carriage. Then he hopped onto the carriage and, with neighbors looking on, triumphantly drove it around. Ford sold the horseless carriage soon after. Already, he

Still in the day of the horse-drawn carriage, onlookers take a skeptical view of Henry Ford and his first gasoline-powered vehicle.

had an idea for a bigger and better engine-powered carriage.

By 1899, Ford had resigned his job at Edison Illuminating to devote full time to his second car. When he finished it late that year, Ford showed the car to a Detroit businessman. The car impressed the man so much that he helped Ford start the Detroit Automobile Company. But the Detroit automobile did not sell, and Ford could not convince his partner to invest more money in the company. It was not reliable, and the public was skeptical of this newfangled machine. In just one year, the Detroit Automobile Company went out of business.

Undaunted, Ford built a stripped-down 26-horsepower race car in 1901. He drove the car in a race that year and won, attracting new investors. One investor was Alexander Malcomson, a Detroit coal merchant. Ford and Malcomson agreed to build a car for the public. Together, the businessmen formed the Ford and Malcomson Company.

Ford's first task was to design a quieter, sturdier engine. The new design impressed John and Horace Dodge, who owned a large machine shop in Detroit. The Dodge brothers agreed to build the car chassis for Ford.

By June 1903, Ford and Malcomson had secured a small manufacturing plant in Detroit. They changed the name to the Ford Motor Company and hired ten workers to assemble the cars. Ford was on his way to becoming the most famous auto maker in the world.

That same month, the first automobile rolled out of the Ford Motor Company. Ford called it the Model A. It had two forward speeds, a reverse gear, and a top speed of 30 MPH. The price of the car was $850. By July, Ford was building 15 cars a day.

Ford worked long hours that first year. Often he helped the workers in the shop. And his efforts soon paid off. By January of 1904, Ford had sold over 658 cars at a profit of $98,851. In the following six months, Ford sold 1,700 cars. By 1905, business had become so good that Ford had outgrown its factory. To keep up with demand, the company constructed a building, which was ten times larger than the original factory.

With the success of the Model A, Ford began looking to the future. He decided to build an inexpensive car that everyone could afford. Not only would the new model be revolutionary, but its manufacturing process would be revolutionary as well—and would help keep costs down.

"The way to make automobiles is to make one automobile like another automobile," Ford said, "to make them all alike, to make them come through the factory all alike, just as one pin is like another when it comes from a pin factory. If you freeze the design and concentrate on production, as the volume goes up, the cars are certain to become cheaper. I mean to turn out a car that workingmen can buy."

Ford called this car the Model T. And it would forever change the face of the nation. The Model T, introduced in 1908, was a marvel of its day. A hood covered the front engine, its four cylinders could produce a top speed of 45 MPH, and it got 20 miles per gallon of gas. Car dealers were amazed. "It is without a doubt the greatest creation in automobiles ever placed before people," one dealer said.

The Ford Model T

The Model T was a huge success. Ford needed more factory space—much more. He began looking around Detroit for a new plant site and found a 60-acre racetrack in Highland Park. Ford decided that he would build the largest car factory in the world there.

Built of concrete, steel, and more than 50,000 square feet of windows, the new Highland Park plant became known as the Crystal Palace. Ford moved into the plant in 1910. There his employees made the Model T on an assembly line. This concept revolutionized car manufacturing and made car ownership possible for the average worker.

Ford had manufactured the Model A in the traditional way. That is, employees assembled each car at one spot on the factory floor. Workers had to bring parts to the assembly spot to build the cars. But with the assembly line, the Model T moved while the workers stayed put. The new model moved past a line of workers who built the car, part by part.

Ford did not invent assembly line manufacturing. That distinction went to Frederick Winslow Taylor who did time-and-motion studies of machine shops in the 1880s, calculating how long it took workers to build things and what they could do to improve performance. Production chief Charles Sorenson suggested the Ford assembly line. And University of Detroit teacher Clarence Avery perfected the technique for Ford. But Henry Ford did make the decision to adopt the process. And in doing so, Ford became an American hero.

With the assembly line, the time needed to build a Model T dropped from 12.5 hours to 2 hours and 38 minutes. By 1913, Ford was selling over 200,000 cars per year. By January 1914, Ford was making a Model T every 93 minutes.

Henry Ford was rich—one of the richest in the nation. But to become wealthy, he had put in many long hours at the office. This did not leave much time for his wife or young son, Edsel. And he often plowed the money he made back into the business.

Ford decided to devote some of his wealth to build a

Workers building cars on an early Ford assembly line

mansion in Dearborn. He selected a 2,000-acre site and
built his dream home, which he called Fair Lane.
Constructed of limestone, Fair Lane had a bowling
alley, an indoor swimming pool, a golf course, and an
artificial lake. Ford's favorite room was the sun porch.
There he spent many hours pursuing another passion:
bird watching.

When World War I erupted in Europe in 1914,
Ford devoted some of his wealth to form a peacemaking
organization at The Hague in Holland. The organization worked to ease tensions between the warring
nations. Germany agreed to talk peace, but the Allies

Henry Ford named his stately home Fair Lane.

(France, Great Britain, and Russia) were not interested in the discussions. In 1917, America entered the war, and Ford's peace organization collapsed. "I wanted to see peace," Ford said. "I at least tried to bring it about. Most men did not even try."

Ford shut down his Model T plant to build ambulances, helmets, shells, armor plate, and airplane motors for America's war effort. Later in the war, Ford built subchasers (ships that chased and destroyed submarines) and tanks.

Just before the war ended, President Woodrow Wilson asked Henry Ford to run for the Senate of the

United States. Because he disliked politics, Ford wasn't thrilled with the idea. But he still felt a need to do what he could for peace. Ford ran as an independent candidate, but he lost to Republican Truman Newbury in a close election.

After the election, Ford returned to what he did best: building cars. He continued making improvements to the Model T, adding a new muffler, a better engine, and electric wiring so it could have headlights. The Model T continued to sell as fast as Ford could produce them. By 1924, the company sold its 10 millionth Ford.

But suddenly, in 1925, sales of the Model T began to decline. Despite the added improvements over the years, the Model T was not keeping up with the competition. Much more expensive cars were doing better than the Model T. These cars had new features like a self-starter that started with the turn of a key and removable tires. The Model T didn't.

Ford's top executives tried to convince Henry Ford that the glory days of the Model T were over and that the company needed to design a new car. But Henry Ford had difficulty letting go of the car that had made him rich and famous. He ignored the advice and insisted on producing more Model T's. Sales continued to decline.

Finally, on May 25, 1927, the Ford Motor Company made a formal announcement that it would build a new car: the second Model A. Henry Ford used the occasion to pay tribute to the Model T.

"The Model T was a pioneer," Ford said to a crowd of reporters. "Things are changing. A newer car is needed. But the Model T will always hold a place in American history for its contributions to social welfare. It had stamina and power. It was the car that ran before there were good roads to run on. It broke down the barriers of distance in rural sections, brought people of these sections closer together. Now we will build a new car. But we are still proud of the Model T Ford."

The next day, Ford rode the last Model T out of the factory—the 15 millionth to be built. Then the company shut down the Model T assembly line for good.

Auto enthusiasts wondered if Ford would be able to top the Model T's success. But when Ford introduced the new Model A on December 2, 1927, the critics praised it. The Model A was lower and more modern than the Model T. It had a quieter, more powerful four-cylinder engine that delivered a top speed of 65 MPH. Moreover, the Model A had an ignition system that started the car with the turn of a key, shock absorbers that made for a smoother ride, and a safety-glass windshield that was difficult to shatter.

The Model A was a tremendous success. By the end of 1928, Ford was producing 6,400 cars per day. In 1929, the company made nearly two million cars.

To make owning a Model A easier, Ford introduced

Ford's new Model A

a revolutionary buying system through its finance company, the Universal Credit Company. Ford would lend money to the buyer who would in turn repay the loan in small monthly amounts. Today, this finance system remains the most popular method of buying a car.

On October 29, 1929, the stock market crashed. This caused a financial panic throughout America. People rushed to their banks to withdraw their money. But most banks did not have enough money to cover all the withdrawals. The "run" on the banks forced many

41

of them to close. Millions of people lost their savings. With no money to spend on consumer goods, many businesses failed. Now people had no money *or* jobs. The Great Depression had begun.

The stock market crash did not personally affect Henry Ford. He and a handful of investors owned Ford Motor Company outright. There was no stock to trade on the market. So, in December 1929, Ford was able to give his employees raises. Ford even posted a $91 million profit.

But the following year, the Great Depression caught up with the Ford Motor Company. Car sales declined, and profits fell to $40 million. In 1931, as the company lost money, Ford had its worst year.

Still, Ford knew he would weather the storm. He introduced a new model: the Ford V-8. It had an eight-cylinder engine, a new transmission, and an incredibly low price tag of $460.

Sales of the V-8 started slowly but increased steadily. By 1934, Ford Motor Company was making money again. But for the first time in history, the Ford workers were unhappy with their pay and with their working conditions. The Depression had forced Ford to cut pay and to increase work time. As a result, the workers decided to form a union.

Ford fought hard to keep the union from forming and he fired anyone who was sympathetic to the union. He had guards search lunch boxes to prevent the spread

The 1932 Ford V-8 and its new engine

of union pamphlets. In May 1937, Ford guards beat union activists from the newly formed United Auto Workers (UAW) who were passing out leaflets at the Ford plant. The incident created a national outrage against Ford. But Ford managed to keep the union out of his factory.

On April 1, 1941, Ford fired eight workers at the Ford plant for union activity. Word spread throughout the Ford empire, and slowly 50,000 workers stopped working. The first Ford strike had begun.

On April 10, Henry Ford reluctantly agreed to permit a vote on the union issue. The workers voted overwhelmingly for a union. The UAW drew up an agreement, setting the conditions between workers and the company. But Ford refused to sign.

Finally, Mrs. Ford stepped in. Tired of all the fighting and turmoil, she told her husband to sign the agreement, or she would leave him. Ford realized that his stubbornness would cost him a lot more than money. Ford and the workers signed the agreement, and the triumphant Ford employees returned to work.

On December 7, 1941, the Japanese attacked the U.S. fleet at Pearl Harbor in Honolulu, Hawaii. Suddenly, the United States was thrust into World War II, which had begun in Europe in 1939.

Ford stopped making cars and turned his factories to the war effort. Ford plants built tanks, trucks, and other war equipment. The company built a new factory at

Warplanes and other weapons built at Ford plants helped the Allies win World War II.

Willow Run near Detroit. The plant was building 650 bombers per month by 1944. But the war took its toll on the Ford family. Ford's son, Edsel, who was now overseeing most of the business, died of stomach cancer on May 26, 1943.

Soon after Edsel's death, Henry Ford's health began to deteriorate rapidly. Ford tried to return to the presidency of the company, but he could not handle the workload. His grandson, Henry Ford II, returned from the navy to assume full responsibility. Henry Ford II proved to be more than capable, as he reorganized the company and installed a modern bookkeeping system. Ford Motor Company's future was secure.

Edsel Ford

On April 7, 1947, while preparing for bed at Fair Lane, Henry Ford experienced a dreadful coughing spell. "My head hurts," he complained to his wife. "My throat's so dry." Clara got him some water and returned to his side. Without warning, Henry Ford died of a stroke at the age of 84.

Henry Ford's car designs did not make him famous. But his use of the assembly line made him immortal. Will Rogers, a popular comedian in Henry Ford's time, said this to the legendary auto maker: "It will take a

Henry Ford II

hundred years to tell whether you have helped us or
hurt us. But you certainly didn't leave us like you found
us."

The brothers Dodge— John (above) and Horace

3

The Dodge Brothers

*T*he Dodge brothers built the American automobile industry. They supplied the chassis (car frames) for Henry Ford's cars. Without the cooperation of the Dodge brothers, Ford may not have become an automobile legend.

John Francis Dodge was born in Niles, Michigan, on October 25, 1864. His brother, Horace Elgin Dodge, entered the world on May 17, 1868. The young Dodge brothers spent long hours in their father's machine shop. There they learned to help him repair and rebuild marine engines.

Although he was not a good student, John finished high school in 1882. After graduation, he went to work in his father's machine shop. Horace spent most of his time there as well and, as a result, his schooling suffered. Horace eventually dropped out of high school just a few months before graduation.

As the Dodge brothers matured, they took over more and more of the decision making at the machine shop. Their father, Daniel, was a good machinist, but he was not a good businessman. Nor was he ambitious. John and Horace did not see much of a future for themselves in Niles. They wanted more out of life than their father's machine shop.

The two brothers left Niles and set out to make their fortune elsewhere. They moved to Port Huron, Michigan, where they hoped to start a machine shop of their own. But they lacked the money necessary to buy new tools, rent workspace, and hire employees. So the Dodge brothers found jobs with a manufacturer of agricultural machines.

Unhappy in Port Huron, the Dodges next moved to Detroit, Michigan. The year was 1886. Although John and Horace were young, their machinist skills were better than men twice their age. Because of this, they secured well-paying jobs at the Murphy Boiler Works. The Dodge brothers prospered at Murphy's, and they were able to live a modest lower-middle-class life. Still, they were not satisfied.

John married Ivy Hawkins on September 22, 1892. He moved out of the house he had shared with Horace and their parents, who had joined them in Detroit, but he stayed in the neighborhood. John and Horace were inseparable in their youth, and their close relationship did not change when they became adults.

Four years later, Horace married Anna Thompson during his lunch break. After the ceremony, Horace returned to Murphy's to finish his daily work. Horace and his bride lived with his mother and father.

After Daniel Dodge died in 1897, John and Horace formed a partnership with businessman Fred S. Evans and started their own business in nearby Windsor, Canada. They called their new venture Evans & Dodge Bicycle Company. They built durable, high-quality bicycles.

Evans & Dodge remained in business for two years. Then the National Cycle and Automobile Company of Canada acquired it and stopped production of the E&D bicycle. But the new owners used Horace's ball bearing design on their own bicycles.

A year after the acquisition, Canadian Cycle and Motor Company of Windsor bought National Cycle. Canadian Cycle paid the Dodge brothers $7,500 for their share of the business, plus a royalty on Horace's ball bearing design.

In 1901, the Dodge brothers took the money and invested it in a business of their own. They bought machinery, hired employees, and rented a building in Detroit. They called their machine company Dodge Brothers.

One of their first jobs was the construction of a few

An early bicycle from the Dodge brothers

automobile engines. Ransom Olds, the founder of the Oldsmobile Corporation, placed the order. This was the first involvement of the Dodge brothers with the industry in which they would one day make their fortunes.

The engines the Dodge brothers built for Oldsmobile were on time and well made. Olds was so pleased with the work that he gave the Dodge brothers a contract to manufacture car transmissions. There was only one problem—Olds wanted 3,000 of them!

The order was huge—one of the biggest in the auto industry at the time. John and Horace had to expand their business immediately or risk losing the contract. So, they purchased $10,000 worth of new equipment and built a new machine shop in Detroit.

The Olds order made Dodge Brothers one of the largest suppliers in the automotive industry. By 1903, car makers had produced 11,000 cars in the United States. Nearly 30 percent were Oldsmobiles—and they all had Dodge transmissions.

The Dodge brothers were making a lot of money. But they plowed most of it back into the business for further expansion. They now had more than 150 employees and a modern factory.

That same year, Henry Ford came to the Dodge brothers, hoping they would build automobile parts for him. The Dodge brothers had to think hard about the request. If they accepted the order, they would have to retool their machinery—and that would cost a lot of money. Besides, Ford Motor Company had just started, and very few people in town had any faith in Henry Ford.

For unknown reasons, John and Horace agreed to make the automobile parts for Ford Motor Company. The contract was worth $162,500. Because Ford was having financial problems, the Dodge brothers agreed to invest $10,000 in Ford Motor Company. In return, they received 100 shares of stock. John Dodge also joined Ford's board of directors.

By early 1904, Ford Motor Company had sold 650

cars. The number was not huge, but Ford was making money. That meant more business for Dodge Brothers.

By early 1905, the Ford Motor Company was experiencing great success. It was building 25 cars per day, and the Dodge brothers had to continually expand their plant to keep up with the demand for parts. By mid-1905, Ford needed enough parts for 400 cars per month.

The relationship between the Dodge brothers and Ford Motor Company was not guaranteed. In fact, as Ford grew more successful, he began looking into the possibility of making his own car parts. Aware of Ford's decision, the Dodge brothers began thinking of ways to protect their business.

In November 1905, Henry Ford started the Ford Manufacturing Company. By 1906, Ford was making his own car engines and chassis. That year, the Dodge brothers supplied only axles and transmissions for the Ford automobiles. They still had all the work they could handle, but they also knew that one day they would lose all of Ford's business.

In the autumn of 1908, Ford Motor Company introduced the Model T. It was one of the biggest success stories in the history of the automobile—and the Dodge brothers were still building parts for it. Once again, the Dodges had to expand their plant to keep up with the demand for parts. By 1909, manufacturers in the United States had built 123,000 cars. One-third of them were Fords with parts manufactured by Dodge Brothers.

In 1910, the Dodge brothers built a new factory in a section of Detroit called Hamtramck. By then, Dodge Brothers was the largest parts-manufacturing firm in the United States. The company added a foundry in 1912 and employed 5,000 people. The company had an annual payroll of over $6 million. John ran the business while Horace designed new equipment and manufacturing systems.

In 1913, the Dodge brothers finally decided to end their business relationship with the Ford Motor Company. The reason for such a major decision was simple: the Dodge brothers wanted to build their own cars.

The news traveled quickly throughout the automotive world. With its reputation as a builder of quality car parts, Dodge had little trouble creating a market for its automobiles. Immediately after the announcement, 22,000 people applied to sell Dodges in their own dealerships. Most people felt that the Dodge would be a success.

One thing was certain: the Dodge brothers could afford the risk. By 1913, their combined worth was over $50 million. They sold $10 million in car parts to Ford each year, and dividends on their Ford stock brought them $3 million in additional yearly revenue.

The Dodge brothers spent long hours designing the car that would bear their name. Horace was responsible for the engine design, and John worked out the details of the car's body. At the time, most auto bodies were made of wood. But John, being a machinist, didn't trust wood and opted for steel instead.

The new Dodge Brothers Motor Car Company began in June 1914. John was president and Horace was vice president. Both were directors of the corporation. They retooled and expanded the factory: new construction cost well over $1 million; the retooling cost about the same. At the same time, the work force increased to 7,500. The Dodge brothers were ready to build their car.

The first Dodge rolled off the 12-man assembly line on November 14, 1914. The brothers gave their car the informal name "Old Betsy." The Dodge came in one color: black. And there was only one model: a five-passenger touring car. In 1915, the company introduced a two-seat roadster.

The Dodge brothers built 249 cars their first year. But by the end of 1915, they had manufactured more than 45,000 Dodges. A new Dodge sold for $785 and was a sturdy, dependable car.

Word spread quickly about the durable Dodge. In 1916, the company sold 70,000; in 1917, 101,000. By the time the company was five years old, it was the

Horace (left rear) and John (beside him) take a drive in the first Dodge car, fresh from their Hamtramck factory. John Dodge's Detroit estate is in the background.

third-largest auto manufacturer in the United States, behind Ford and General Motors.

By the autumn of 1919, the Dodge brothers were among the richest men in America. John began to build a mansion on the waterfront in Grosse Pointe—a house with 110 rooms, 24 bathrooms, and an exterior of varicolored granite. John wanted his home to be the biggest and best in Detroit.

In January 1920, when the mansion was nearly completed, 56-year-old John Dodge fell ill with respiratory problems. His lungs weakened quickly, then gave out completely. He slipped into a coma and never recovered. On January 4, 1920, John Dodge died. His sudden death devastated Horace, who would never be able to recover from the terrible loss.

John Dodge's funeral was a great public event. Detroit flew all the flags on its public buildings at half-mast, and a host of prominent businessmen were in attendance. After a long ceremony, his family buried John Dodge in a mausoleum in the Woodlawn Cemetery. Dodge's Grosse Pointe mansion was never finished and it stood vacant before it was finally demolished in 1941.

After his brother's funeral, Horace took his family to Palm Beach, Florida. Horace's health slowly deteriorated throughout the year. Like his brother, Horace had trouble with his lungs. In December, he developed pneumonia. He died on the night of December 10, 1920, with his son and wife at his side.

The story of the Dodge brothers holds a valuable lesson. It plainly illustrates the virtues of working hard, taking risks, and—most importantly—providing quality. Had the Dodge brothers ignored these virtues, they undoubtedly would not have gone beyond the grimy machine shops that gave birth to their great American dream.

*Ferdinand Porsche at the wheel of his Lohner Porsche car,
1902. His father, Anton (holding child), and brother Oskar
sit behind him.*

4

Ferdinand Porsche

*F*erdinand Porsche was born on September 30, 1875, in Bohemia, which is now a part of the Czech Republic. Ferdinand was a rebellious young man. His father, Anton, wanted him to become a tinsmith and carry on the family business. But the smoke, fire, and gloom of his father's workshop did not interest young Ferdinand. He saw wonders in another world—the magical realm of electricity.

In 1890, when Ferdinand was 15 years old, he asked his father to buy him a ' battery. Ferdinand wanted to conduct electrical experiments in the loft of his family's home in Reichenberg.

Anton became furious. He called electricity "nonsense" and forbade his son from anything that did not concern the tinsmith's craft. Ferdinand's father could not understand why his son wanted to experiment with electricity. He wondered how Ferdinand even knew it existed! Reichenberg was a small peasant town filled with artisans, weavers, carpenters, and tailors. Reichenberg did not even have electricity!

Despite his father's sharp objections, Ferdinand remained determined. He got the battery on his own and began his electrical experiments at night (after working 12-hour days in the tinsmith shop).

Because Anton often worked in distant villages, he was at first unaware of his son's experiments. This gave Ferdinand the opportunity he needed. But one day, Anton stumbled upon Ferdinand's secret. Enraged, Anton stamped on the batteries, smashing them. He did not know that they contained acid. The acid squirted out and burned his boots and skin.

Anton wanted to punish his rebellious son. But Ferdinand's mother, Anna, rescued him. She insisted that Ferdinand had a special talent beyond the tinsmith shop and suggested they send Ferdinand to a special school in Vienna. Anton refused. He pointed out that Reichenberg had a technical school. Ferdinand could go to night classes and work in the shop during the day. Then they would find out if Ferdinand was truly talented. This news overjoyed Ferdinand. Now he could become somebody besides the son of a tinsmith. He had the opportunity to prove his worth and quickly impressed his father.

One night as Anton made his way home from a neighboring village, he saw a strange glow coming from his neighborhood. Fearfully, he rushed home—perhaps his home was burning! But to his delight he discovered that the light was electricity. Ferdinand had built and installed a complete electrical system. It had a generator, switchboard, wires—everything!

The Porsche household was the envy of the neighborhood. Only the Ginzkey carpet factory had electric lights. A few days later, the Ginzkey family approached Anton. They offered to send Ferdinand to Vienna to work as a student employee at Bela Egger, a company that manufactured electrical equipment and machinery. Besides working there, Ferdinand would become a part-time student at the technical university. Thus, he could obtain a better education.

Given what Ferdinand had done to their home, Anton now recognized his son's talent. With his father's blessing, 18-year-old Ferdinand went to Vienna. He had a talent for solving technical problems and excelled at Bela Egger. In just four years, he became the manager of their test department.

At the same time, a Viennese businessman—Jacob Lohner—began looking for someone to help him build electric cars. Lohner owned Jacob Lohner & Company, which built horse-drawn carriages. But Lohner was convinced that electric cars would soon replace carriages as a means of transportation. Electric motors were quiet and clean; internal combustion engines were noisy and smoky. He was certain the public would agree.

In 1898, Lohner hired Porsche to work for him in his newly formed car manufacturing department. Porsche proved to be the bright young star Lohner had hoped he would be. But Porsche also cost Lohner a lot of money since he liked to build many different *prototypes*. (A prototype is an experimental model that attempts to improve existing designs.) But by the autumn of 1899, Porsche had settled on one design.

Lohner and Porsche displayed their first electric car at the 1900 World Exhibition in Paris. Arc lights lit the entire exhibition, which featured an Electricity Palace. The car exhibit was extremely popular. Crowding around these newfangled machines, people stared in wonder. Some cars had petroleum-powered engines; others offered steam-powered engines. But Porsche's electric car was the hit of the show.

The car, called the Lohner-Porsche Chaise, looked a lot like a carriage. It had a central lamp in the front that acted as a headlight. The wheels had wooden spokes and solid rubber tires. Behind the passenger seat was a servant seat. And, astoundingly, electric motors were fitted into the hubs of the wheels. Porsche had built the first front-wheel drive car!

Porsche's electric car had other innovative features. Beside the rear-wheel mechanical brakes, the car had

Twenty-five-year-old Ferdinand Porsche's first car, the 1900 Lohner-Porsche

electric brakes in the front. And since it was powered by electric motors in the wheel hubs, it required no transmission.

The car had two forward speeds: low and high. At low speed, the car traveled at 11 MPH. At high speed, the car could go 23 MPH. For racing purposes, mechanics could adjust the car to travel 37 MPH. Already, Porsche was thinking about auto racing.

The Lohner-Porsche Chaise also had its drawbacks. The car had a "limited range": it could only travel short distances before it lost power. And recharging or replacing its batteries took a long time.

Still, Porsche's electric car was the talk of the exhibition. Its design created worldwide interest. When experts asked Jacob Lohner about the designer, Lohner replied: "He is very young. But he is a man with a big career before him. You will hear of him again."

After the exhibition, Porsche drove the racing version of the Lohner-Porsche Chaise on Semmering Road near Vienna. At the time, Semmering Road was the best-known speed test for cars and motorcycles. Porsche took 14 minutes and 52.5 seconds to finish the six-mile course, setting a record for all types of electric cars. (The previous record was 23 minutes and 27 seconds.)

Ferdinand (steering) in his Lohner-Porsche racing car after his record-setting drive at Semmering

The result pleased Porsche, but he was not happy about his car's limited range. So, he came up with a design that combined the range of the petrol engine with the quiet electric front-wheel drive.

Porsche replaced the heavy batteries in the rear with an internal combustion engine. He fitted a dynamo (generator) to the engine to convert mechanical energy into electricity. Then the electricity powered the hub motors. Porsche called this innovation the "petro-electric mixed car."

The experts remained skeptical. They thought that the hub motors were unnecessary. But Porsche did not want to give up the unique and quiet design. At the Exelberg races in 1902, Porsche drove his mixed car to victory in the 1,000-kg class. Impressed with the performance, the German army purchased the Lohner-Porsche car. So did the Vienna fire brigade, which was one of the first to become motorized.

Though Porsche was known for his intense work habits, he was not totally devoted to the automobile. Porsche also had strong ties to family and took care of his parents, brothers, and sisters. He even treated close friends as family.

While in Vienna, Porsche met Aloisia Johanna Kaes, who worked as a bookkeeper at an electrical plant. She was interested in cars and often attended motor races. When Porsche and Kaes married, they looked forward to the future together and planned to start a family.

By now, Porsche was recognized as one of Austria's most brilliant auto designers. But Jacob Lohner's small manufacturing plant restricted Porsche's growth. As he grew increasingly frustrated over limited budgets and manufacturing capabilities, his relationship with Lohner soured.

In 1905, when he was 30 years old, Porsche left Jacob Lohner & Company to become the technical director for Austrian Daimler in Wiener-Neustadt. At the time, Austrian Daimler was the largest car maker in Austria.

In his new job, Porsche concentrated on passenger and racing car design and continued to find new ways to improve auto performance. He built an 85-horsepower racing car with liquid-cooled rear brakes. And he designed a 32-horsepower passenger car with a four-speed transmission and chain or shaft drive that powered the wheels. The car also had a rear-mounted, 15-gallon gas tank for long trips.

On the home front, the Porsches had two children. First came a daughter, Louise. Then they had a son, Ferry. Ferry would one day follow his father's lead in the auto industry by establishing a company called Porsche.

By 1910, Porsche saw the potential of the airplane. He designed and built aircraft engines—even though Austria did not have a single plane. A 1912 design was an air-cooled, four-cylinder engine with overhead valves. The cylinders on each side angled toward each other in a slight "V" shape—a design found in most of today's auto engines.

Since airplane engines were being constructed, Austria quickly built its air force. By 1913, it had 102 planes—the sixth largest air force in the world. Experts agreed that Porsche airplane engines were the best among the Central European powers.

This was not good news for the rest of Europe. In 1914, World War I erupted. Austria and its German ally had one of the top mechanical engineers on their side. Because of Austria's war effort, Porsche had to forgo auto design temporarily and turn his talents to the development of weapons. He designed a motor-driven cannon with four-wheel drive that enabled the artillery units to follow the army and enter battle quickly. Porsche also designed engines for smaller guns.

By 1916, Porsche was the managing director of the Austrian Daimler company. That same year, Vienna's technical university gave him an honorary doctorate for his engineering work, and the Austrian emperor presented Porsche with a medal for his design work to help the war effort.

After the war, Porsche resumed his auto design work. In 1922, he built his first small car, the Sascha, which had four cylinders and a top speed of 89 MPH.

Porsche now turned his attention to building faster cars. He wanted to make Daimler's Austrian factory famous through auto racing, but the board of directors did not share his view; they saw auto racing as expensive and dangerous.

Frustrated, Porsche decided to join the Daimler branch in Stuttgart, Germany. There, Porsche's ambitions were met favorably. In nine months, he developed a supercharged car for Mercedes, which was part of Daimler.

In 1924, Porsche sent the supercharged Mercedes to the world-famous *Targa Florio* race in Sicily. The Italian Alfa Romeos had dominated the four-lap race for years. Again, racing experts favored the Alfa Romeos to win.

An Alfa Romeo won the first lap. But Porsche's supercharged Mercedes pulled ahead in the second lap. The Alfa Romeo began catching up in the third lap, and the Italians were confident they would win. But the

The 1922 Sascha

Mercedes was too fast. It finished in record time, averaging 41 MPH. Ferdinand Porsche was there to receive the winning prize.

When he returned to Stuttgart, the entire town came out to greet him. People mobbed the town square as the mayor publicly congratulated Porsche. Later, the technical college of Stuttgart made him an honorary doctor.

Despite his success, Porsche began having difficulty at Daimler. He no longer had complete design control, and the board of directors did not receive many of his new ideas—including a small car design—very well. When Daimler suggested that Porsche take a long study trip to the United States, Porsche decided it was time to move on.

In 1929, Steyr Works of Austria hired Porsche as chief engineer. They also made him a member of the board of directors. Porsche designed a large eight-cylinder car called the Austria. Later that year, he drove it to the Paris Salon—the oldest motor show in the world. There the viewers received the Austria with enthusiasm.

Pleased with the results of the Paris show, Porsche returned to his hotel in good spirits. But then he learned that Daimler, now called Daimler-Benz, was about to buy the Steyr company. To Porsche's surprise, he would be working for his former employer once again!

Porsche spent a few months working for Daimler-Benz. But, disliking his limited authority, he soon decided that he did not want to be part of any large auto manufacturer. Only one option was left: to start his own design company.

Because he had a villa in Stuttgart, Porsche decided to form his company there. He hired a commercial manager, Adolf Rosenberger, to run the business. Then he hired a staff of engineers.

Porsche was open for business on December 1, 1930. Immediately, the young company got into financial trouble. Design projects often extended beyond their budgets. He was forced to pay engineers' salaries in installments.

Porsche and his engineers designed their first automobile for the Wanderer firm in Chemnitz, Germany. The medium-size car, called the Wanderer, had a six-cylinder engine. When it became popular, Wanderer ordered an eight-cylinder version of the car. Porsche built a prototype, but the car never saw production. Ferdinand Porsche used the prototype as his own touring car.

In 1931, Zundapp Works in Nurnberg, Germany, decided they needed a small car to offset their slumping motorcycle sales. Since they lacked auto design experience, Zundapp approached Porsche. Thrilled, Porsche used a small car design from his Austrian Daimler days. Counsellor Neumeyer, the owner of Zundapp Works, already had a name for the car. He called it "Volks-auto"—the "people's car." Porsche built three proto-types in 1932. All three had a rear engine, a two-door body, and a spare wheel in the front.

While Porsche's dream of a small car was finally tak-ing shape, a Russian delegation of engineers approached Porsche and invited him to Russia. "We would like you to judge for yourself the possibilities which exist in a country that has unlimited space and inexhaustible resources of wealth," they said.

Porsche was stunned, but interested. What did these Russians want?

Porsche traveled to Russia via train. He visited Kiev, Kursk, and Odessa. He saw factories, foundries, tanks, cars, and airplanes. And the Russians treated him like royalty. But he still did not know what they wanted.

When Porsche arrived in Moscow, he finally got his answer. The Russians did not want him just to design cars for them, they wanted *him!* They offered him a contract to be in charge of their auto industry, tank pro-duction, and electrical works. All Russia's vast resources—and its millions of workers—would be at his disposal. His title would be "State Designer of Russia."

There was more. The Bank of Moscow would finance any research project he developed. All his engi-neering hopes and dreams would be realized. All he had to do was sign the contract.

The offer seemed too good to be true. However,

Porsche would need government permission to leave Russia, his contacts with Germany would be cut off, and he could not build his small people's car or race cars. The typical Russian citizen could not afford a small car. And the country had little interest in racing cars.

From an engineering point of view, the offer was the chance of a lifetime. But Porsche was more than an engineer. He was a family man with strong ties to Germany. In the end, he politely turned down the Russian offer. The next day, Porsche returned to Stuttgart and his struggling design business. He devoted much time developing race cars for Germany's Auto-Union company, some of which set racing records.

On January 30, 1933, Rosenberger, the commercial manager of Porsche's company, resigned and left for America. Porsche continued working on the people's car. But later that year, the motorcycle business revived. Production increased so much that the company had no time to build the Volksauto. Once again Porsche shelved his dream of a small car.

But at the beginning of 1934, the project was suddenly revived. Porsche was called to the Chancellery in Berlin to meet with Adolf Hitler. Hitler wanted Porsche to design a car that the people of Germany could buy for less than 1,000 marks. It would be called "Volkswagen."

Porsche redesigned his small car. It would have a

four-cylinder engine, a maximum speed of 62 MPH, and get 36 miles to the gallon. Porsche's company built the first prototypes in 1936, and the German government tested them relentlessly throughout 1937. Porsche's sturdy design held up. Now the time had come to go into mass production.

Having accomplished his task, Porsche decided to take a trip to the United States. There he visited legendary car maker Henry Ford. Porsche told Ford all about the Volkswagen program. Then he invited Ford to visit German auto makers. Ford shook his head. He did not see how a trip would be possible because war was about to break out in Europe.

In Stuttgart, Porsche admires his Series 30 Volkswagen (1937).

Ford's comment stunned Porsche. War? In Europe? He did not understand how Ford could say such a thing. Because political matters did not interest Porsche, he was not fully aware of the tense political scene in his own backyard. All he ever wanted to do was design and build cars.

When Porsche returned to Stuttgart, Daimler-Benz approached him about a different sort of project. Daimler wanted Porsche to design a car that would shatter the land speed record that stood at 309 MPH.

Porsche designed his super car with three axles—one in the front and two in the back. The V-12 engine was behind the driver's seat. The car was 29 feet long with tail fins, weighed 2.8 tons, and was designed to travel over 400 MPH. But the super car never saw production. Henry Ford's fear about a war in Europe came true and prevented its final development.

Before World War II began, Porsche was hard at work on another pet project. He wanted to design a people's tractor that most farmers could afford. But the war interfered with those plans too. Porsche had to turn his talents to military designs. He placed the tractor program in the capable hands of his son, Ferry.

Porsche designed two famous tanks: the Tiger and the Ferdinand. Both tanks had air-cooled engines—a Porsche trademark. Moreover, he fitted the Tiger with special armor that enhanced its fearsome presence on the battlefield.

A third tank, dubbed the "Mouse," was, in fact, the largest tank ever built. It weighed 180 tons and had impenetrable armor plating. Slow and hard to maneuver—often too heavy to cross bridges—the tank *did* work. However, it never went into full production because Porsche designed it toward the end of the war when Allied bombers pounded German manufacturing to a standstill.

Porsche's beloved Stuttgart was a frequent Allied target. To protect him, the German government transferred Porsche's design office from Stuttgart to the primitive town of Gmünd, Austria, which was not connected to the railway system. There Porsche designed in an old barracks while cows grazed nearby.

In June 1945, the United States Army captured Porsche and sent him to a castle in Hessen. There, they interrogated him. Afterwards, the army allowed him to return to his villa.

Just when Porsche thought his life would return to

Porsche's 1944 Mouse tank—the largest ever built

normal, the French arrested him and sent him to Paris. French officials gave no reason for his arrest, but clearly Porsche played a vital role in arming Germany's war machine.

In Paris, the French held him in the porter's lodge of a villa belonging to Renault, a French car manufacturer. The company sought Porsche's opinion numerous times to help improve its automobiles.

After being transferred to a prison in Dijon, France, Porsche was finally released on August 5, 1947. On returning to his villa, Porsche assisted with a race car design for the Cisitalia works in Turin, Italy. His son, Ferry, and Porsche's chief engineer, Karl Rabe, had started the design while Porsche was in prison. When he examined the design, Porsche declared, "If I had designed it, I would not have done it any differently."

Unfortunately, the Cisitalia never saw a race because of financial difficulties. Then an Argentine company, Autoar, bought Cisitalia. But Autoar had trouble running and maintaining the car, and eventually abandoned it.

In 1947, Porsche and his son went to work on the first car to carry the Porsche name. Its distinctive design would set the standard for all future Porsche cars. The Porsche prototype, called the 356, was actually a sports car version of the Volkswagen Porsche had designed for Adolf Hitler. Ready in 1948, the Porsche 356 was an open two-seater, with a maximum speed of

86 MPH. Porsche placed a Volkswagen engine in the rear and the fuel tank in front with the spare tire.

Auto experts gave rave reviews to the Porsche 356. Orders came in from all over the world. But one problem made the fulfilling of these orders almost impossible: Porsche's Gmünd factory had a very small staff, and the town was not even connected to a railroad!

In the winter of 1948-49, small-scale production began. The company built five cars per month. All body work was done by hand—by one man! When he did not work, production stopped. This slow process lasted for six months. Then Porsche hired more people until he employed nearly 300 workers. Production increased, but so did the orders.

At Gmünd in 1948, Ferry Porsche and his father stand next to the first car to bear the family name, the Porsche 356.

Next, Porsche approached the mayor of Stuttgart and asked permission for his company to return to its old production plant. The military government, run by the Allies, granted Porsche's request.

Porsche's return to Stuttgart was completed in 1950. The company built 8 to 10 cars per month. Eventually, Porsche would produce 80 cars per month from the same factory.

Porsche's reputation for high performance and high quality grew, and exports began to soar. Sports car enthusiasts from around the world could not stop talking about the 356. The Porsche legacy had begun.

On September 30, 1950, Ferdinand Porsche celebrated his 75th birthday. Porsche owners from all over Germany flooded the streets of Stuttgart, honking their horns and flashing their lights in honor of the great car designer. Deeply touched, Porsche emerged from his villa and walked from car to car, personally thanking each driver.

The tribute proved to be timely. In 1951, Porsche suffered a crippling stroke from which he never recovered. On January 30, 1952, Ferdinand Porsche died. Hundreds came to mourn him at his funeral.

Ferdinand Porsche was truly one of the world's greatest auto designers, a man whose love for automobiles had helped him forge a long and successful career. His death marked the end of an era of the great auto designers—an era in which one person could visualize and create a car through each step of the manufacturing process.

The modern auto industry owes much to this brilliant man. Innovations like front-wheel drive, air-cooled engines, and V-shaped engines remain standards of automobiles today because of their efficiency and performance. Thanks to Porsche's son, Ferry, who continued Ferdinand's tradition of excellence, many of the most popular cars today still bear the Porsche name. The classic shapes of the Porsche 911, 928, and 959 still symbolize Ferdinand Porsche's dedication to innovation, performance, and quality.

The sleek Porsche 959

*Motorcycles, not cars, most interested young William Lyons,
here aboard one in the early 1920s.*

82

5

William Lyons and Jaguar

*T*hroughout its long history, the Jaguar company has produced some of the most exciting and sophisticated auto designs ever. Its founder, William Lyons, was both a sports car pioneer and an innovator. William Lyons was born on September 4, 1901, in Blackpool, England. His parents hoped that one day Lyons would take over the family's music shop, where he sold musical intruments and sheet music. But young Lyons had other ideas. He had become deeply interested in motorcycles.

After receiving his education, Lyons joined the firm of Crossley Motors as a trainee. But Lyons was unhappy at Crossley in Manchester and returned to Blackpool. There he helped with the family business and worked at two different garages.

In 1920, Lyons met William Walmsley, who manufactured sidecars for motorcycles. Walmsley's work
impressed Lyons, who suggested that he come to work
for Walmsley as a designer. Walmsley agreed. Soon
the two were producing eight to ten sidecars each
week in Walmsley's garage.

In 1922, Walmsley and Lyons formed the Swallow
Sidecar Company. The organization that would one
day become Jaguar had begun. Swallow moved into a
workshop in Blackpool and immediately hired several
workers. Soon, the company was turning out high-
quality sidecars with a comfortable seat and plenty of

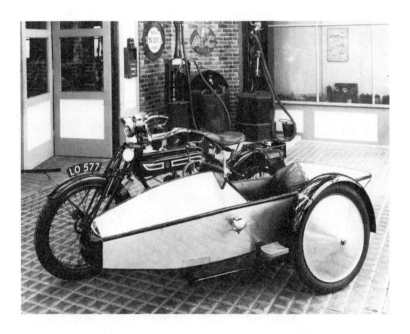

The 1928 Swallow Model 4 Super Sports Side Car

legroom. In 1926, the company became the Swallow Sidecar and Coachbuilding Company. The Swallow sidecars became well known and respected, but the automobile was becoming a more popular means of transportation. Reacting to this trend, Lyons quickly designed and built a wooden auto body that he bolted to the frame of a little Austin Seven car. Lyons built more Austin Swallows. In 1928, the company moved to Coventry, and the Austin-Swallow was in demand.

In 1930, Lyons introduced the Standard-Swallow.

An Austin-Swallow

It was a four-seater with wire wheels and a large, chrome-plated grill that allowed plenty of air to flow into the engine. The Standard-Swallow became an instant sensation. With the success of the Standard behind him, Lyons made plans to build his own cars.

In 1932, Swallow introduced its first car: the SS1. It had a wooden body with steel panels and a top speed of 70 MPH. It also came with a stiff price tag, but auto enthusiasts loved it. By 1935, Swallow was building nearly 2,000 cars per year. The SS1 models were so popular that Swallow stopped building auto bodies on chassis from other manufacturers. In 1934, the company changed its name again. Now Lyons called his company SS Cars Ltd. The following year, Lyons introduced a line of cars called Jaguars. Ten years later, in 1945, Jaguar became the new name of his company

Lyons assured the public that the new SS Jaguars would be logical improvements of the popular SS1. In October 1935, Lyons introduced his first four-door sedan. Though the SS Jaguar was built with the family in mind, it still offered sporty high performance and character. The SS Jaguar had a top speed of 90 MPH. The most notable change was the body, which was all-steel construction.

Lyons was pleased with his new car, but he was determined to build a 100-MPH sports car. He had the Standard six-cylinder engine redesigned for 30 more horsepower and placed it in the Standard frame. The SS 100 Jaguar was born.

The two-door SS 100 had a roomy and luxurious interior—a Jaguar trademark. The bucket seats were top-grain cowhide, and the dashboard was constructed of genuine walnut. The driver could even store luggage behind the seats.

Lyons tested his new sports car at many road rallies and races all over Great Britain and Europe. In 1937, an SS 100 won the International Vila Real race. The Royal Automobile Club awarded the SS 100 the "Best Performance" award. In 1937 and 1938, an SS 100 captured the Manufacturers Team Prize in the Royal Automobile Club Rally. Production of all SS Jaguars grew to more than 12,000 per year—a remarkable feat, considering that workers built all Jaguars by hand.

World War II brought a sudden halt to Jaguar production. The company's factory in Coventry, England, retooled to manufacture airplane wings, cockpit roofs, bomb doors, tanks, military sidecars, and light scout trucks.

By March 1945, Lyons was making plans for the new Jaguars. He decided, however, to drop the initials "SS," which reminded people of Nazi Germany's dreaded SS soldiers during World War II. In March 1945 the company became Jaguar Cars Ltd.

Following the war, Jaguar brought out new designs quickly. The war had been tough on the automobile industry, but now people were ready to buy. By 1947, Jaguar was producing 4,342 cars per year for customers all over the world.

At the London Motor Show in 1948, Lyons introduced a new sports car: the XK 120 roadster, which became the hit of the show. The XK 120's design was an eye-opener. It had sleek, aerodynamic lines with a long, low hood and a luxurious interior. Even more, the car had a top speed of 120 MPH.

Word of the XK 120's looks and performance spread quickly. Orders came in from all over the world. Production could not keep up with demand, and customers had to put their names on a waiting list. By late 1949, the XK 120 was the most wanted car in America. Two other versions, the XK 140 and the XK 150, were built from 1955 to 1961. In all, the company constructed nearly 34,000 XK's, making it one of Jaguar's most successful models.

In 1950, Jaguar introduced one of its all-time classic luxury cars: the Jaguar Mark VII. The company unveiled the car at motor shows in London and New York and caused an instant sensation.

The Mark VII was a large, heavy sedan. It was ten feet long and over six feet wide, making it one of the largest luxury vehicles of its time. But what made this car a classic was its performance: The Mark VII had a top speed of 103 MPH and could travel from 0 to 60 MPH in 13.4 seconds.

Above: Hollywood star Clark Gable steps into a Jaguar XK 120. Below: the regal Jaguar Mark VII

Although Jaguar intended the Mark VII as a high-performance family car, the company also entered it in a number of rallies and races. In the early 1950s, the Mark VII won a series of Monte Carlo rallies. It was so powerful that it could easily plow through the deep snow drifts that the drivers often encountered. The Mark VII also won the Silverstone Production Car Race in 1953.

The year 1950 also began Jaguar's first organized effort to develop a racing car. The success and power of the XK 120 convinced Lyons that he had the beginnings of a race car that could eventually compete with the likes of Ferrari and Mercedes-Benz. Lyons decided that Jaguar would build a car that could win one of the world's most famous races: the 24-hour race at Le Mans. Jaguar's response was the C-Type, which had a maximum speed of 150 MPH and could go from 0 to 60 MPH in 7 seconds.

The C-Type was ready by 1951. Jaguar entered three C-Types in Le Mans. After all three led during the early hours, two C-Types broke down. But the third went on to capture the race, averaging 98.5 MPH. A C-Type also had the fastest lap at 105.2 MPH.

The C-Types had difficulty in 1952, however, and were forced from the race. But in 1953, they returned with a vengeance, finishing first, second, and fourth.

The D-Type Jaguar replaced the C-Type in 1954.

It was a much improved race car with a top speed of
170 MPH. The D-Type finished second at Le Mans
that year. But the car went on to capture first place in
1955, 1956, and 1957.

Because of Jaguar's incredible racing success and
post-war exports, Queen Elizabeth II knighted
William Lyons in 1956. During that decade, Lyons
had brought Jaguar to the heights of the sports car
world, and Jaguar had become a source of pride to an
entire nation.

In 1957, a major fire at the Jaguar factory halted

*The D-Type Jaguar crosses the finish line first in the 12-
hour race at Reims, France, in 1954. This was the first racing win for the D-Type.*

further development of Jaguar race cars. Throughout the late 1950s, people wondered if Jaguar would be able to top its earlier success with the C-Type and D-Type race cars.

In March 1961, Lyons had the answer: the XK-E. The company introduced the Jaguar XK-E (or E-Type) roadster at the Geneva Auto Show. The car had the best features of the D-Type plus new features. Car enthusiasts went wild for the XK-E, which had a top

The E-Type Jaguar gleams on display at the 1961 New York Auto Show.

Donald Gresham Stokes, given the title Lord Stokes by Queen Elizabeth in 1969, began his career with Britain's Leyland Motors in 1930.

speed of 150 MPH and could go from 0 to 60 MPH in 6.5 seconds. Even more, it averaged 17 miles per gallon—something unheard of in the early 1960s. At the time, the XK-E was the fastest sports car in the world. By the mid-1960s, it had become the most famous.

In 1966, Lyons decided to merge his company with the giant British Motor Corporation (B.M.C.) to form British Motor Holdings (B.M.H). Lyons believed that such a merger would ensure the continued success of his company well into the future. Yet it nearly brought the proud company to extinction.

B.M.H. already had financial problems when it merged with Jaguar. In 1968, Lord Stokes of Leyland bought B.M.H. and formed a new company—British Leyland. Jaguar's problems were just beginning.

That same year, Lyons introduced his final automobile: the XJ6. This luxury car had a top speed of 124 MPH and could go from 0 to 60 MPH in only 8.8 seconds. Auto experts named the XJ6 "Car of the

The Jaguar XJ6

Year," as it set new standards in both luxury and performance.

Orders for the XJ6 flowed in from all over the world. Waiting lists grew longer and longer. But while the XJ6 enjoyed success, British Leyland was slowly falling apart. Many of its key managers were retiring, and although Jaguar still turned a profit, British Leyland's other ventures were failing.

In 1972, when William Lyons retired from Jaguar,

Sir William Lyons died at his home, Wappenbury Hall, Warwickshire, England, on February 8, 1985.

British Leyland was sputtering. To save it from total collapse, the British government took control.

Jaguar quality suffered during the 1970s when the company tried to cut costs. As a result, the name noted for quality was tarnished, and auto sales continued to dive. In 1975, the company placed its future on a new model: the XJ-S. A total of 14,792 XJ-S units were built, the last in 1981.

By the early 1980s, car production at Jaguar was only 14,000 per year. But because quality control was improving, Jaguar's image was being restored. When the company introduced a series of XJ models throughout the 1980s, it increased Jaguar's profitability. Production of one model, the XJ-S, could not keep up with demand.

In 1986, Jaguar introduced the car that led to the rebirth of the Jaguar legend. Called the new XJ6, it had a top speed of 136 MPH. This model could go from 0 to 60 MPH in 9.6 seconds. Within weeks of its introduction, the waiting list in Great Britain was over one year. The response in the United States was equally enthusiastic.

The XJ6 has led Jaguar's resurgence into the 1990s. Once again, the company has become famous for style, performance, and quality. In 1990, Ford of Europe purchased Jaguar, assuring its continued success well into the decade.

From the beginning, William Lyons strove to build

elegant but powerful automobiles. That rare combination of performance and style remains in today's Jaguars. Although it is owned by one of the largest auto makers in the world, Jaguar still maintains its identity and strict standards for design and quality.

Alfred P. Sloan, Jr., brought sound business management practices and strong executive leadership to a young automobile industry and turned General Motors into one of the largest, most profitable companies in the world.

6

Alfred Sloan and General Motors

*T*his success story is not about revolutionary auto designs or super fast sports cars. It is about the making of a business giant—General Motors.

Alfred Sloan had no secret ambitions to become a race car driver. Nor did he have a talent for exotic automobile designs. Sloan was good—very good—at organizing. He used his talents to forge a collection of companies, not car parts, into one smooth-running machine—a machine that became the largest automobile manufacturer in the world.

Alfred P. Sloan, Jr., was born on May 23, 1875, in New Haven, Connecticut. His father, a prosperous businessman, imported coffee and tea. Sloan grew up in a comfortable home and attended the Brooklyn public schools in New York City. A studious young man, he developed a talent for math and science.

Sloan enrolled in the Brooklyn Polytechnic Institute and graduated a year ahead of his class. He passed the entrance exams for the Massachusetts Institute of Technology (MIT), but the school refused his admission because he was too young. The following year, however, MIT did admit 17-year-old Sloan. Graduating in three years, he received his bachelor's degree in electrical engineering in 1895.

Sloan seemed to have a brilliant future ahead of him. But in 1895, the country was experiencing an economic depression and jobs were hard to find. Sloan, however, managed to secure a position as a designer at the Hyatt Roller Bearing Company in Newark, New Jersey. John Wesley Hyatt, a self-trained inventor who lacked a technical education, ran the company. He had invented celluloid—the first plastic. Hyatt hoped to build his fortune by making plastic billiard balls. But Sloan saw the company's real future in the metal ball bearings it produced. At the time, U.S. industry was rapidly becoming mechanized. Wherever metal turned on metal, ball bearings were needed. That meant nearly everywhere.

Designing a quality ball bearing to withstand the increasing strains of a mechanized industry was not an easy task. Knowledge of scientific principles was needed—something that Hyatt did not have. Consequently, his ball bearing designs were not totally successful, and the company was struggling financially. When a chief investor, John Searles, grew tired of all the financial problems and withdrew his support, Sloan's father stepped in and invested $5,000 to keep the company running. Then he installed his 26-year-old son as president and general manager. But young Sloan's position remained uneasy because his father gave him only six months to turn the company around.

Sloan went to work. He cut costs, raised production, and installed a system of controls and procedures. By the time the six-month deadline arrived, the Hyatt company showed a $12,000 profit.

Near the turn of the century, Sloan realized that the blossoming automobile industry could become his most important customer. Every car rolled. Every engine turned. Every auto manufacturer, therefore, needed steel ball bearings.

Sloan kept a close eye on the auto industry. When a new manufacturer opened its doors, Sloan would send a letter, offering to supply steel bearings.

Olds Motor Company became Sloan's first major customer. In 1899, Sloan wrote to Henry Ford. Soon afterward, Ford Motor Company began buying Hyatt's bearings.

Sloan's organization skills were the key to Hyatt's success. The company could produce customized bearings and deliver them on time. This was critical in the auto industry, where assembly could not start until all parts were on hand. Efficiency was most important to Sloan. He developed a reputation for driving his work force hard. And the Hyatt company plowed its profits back into the business so it could expand its factory and keep up with the growing demand.

By 1915, automobile sales had soared to over $800,000. Most of this was due to the success of Henry Ford's legendary Model T. Hyatt was still selling steel bearings to Ford, which by now was its biggest customer.

Despite Hyatt's success, however, Sloan grew concerned that another client, General Motors (GM), might produce its own bearings. "I had put my whole life's energy into Hyatt," Sloan said. "Everything I had earned was there in bricks, machinery, and materials." Sloan converted the original factory into a 750,000-square-foot plant that turned out 40,000 bearings a day. But Sloan feared that Hyatt's days were numbered. If Hyatt lost GM's business, the "company would be in a desperate situation," Sloan said.

One day in 1916, the founder and chairman of GM, William Durant, invited Sloan to lunch and offered to buy Hyatt. Sloan saw the offer as an opportunity to multiply his wealth and power and to join a vastly larger organization. After negotiating, Sloan and Hyatt settled on a $13.5 million purchase price.

General Motors merged Hyatt with United Motors Corporation, and Sloan became its president. Sloan did

William C. Durant founded the General Motors Company in 1908.

so well, GM promoted him to vice president and member of the GM executive committee.

In 1920, GM began experiencing trouble due to quality control. By 1921, sales had fallen dramatically, from a 1919 peak of 52,000 cars to a dismal 11,862 units. Then the DuPont family, which owned a major share of General Motors, made a drastic move. They forced William Durant out of his job. Because the new president, Pierre Samuel DuPont, knew nothing about

Workers lower a car body by chain onto the chassis (1920)

cars he, appointed Sloan vice president in charge of operations.

General Motors was a mess. The management team was unorganized. The company was producing ten different lines of cars, including Chevrolet, Oldsmobile, Buick, and Cadillac. Many of these lines competed against each other, and none of the lines had any production planning. Each division simply built as many cars as it could. Then the company hoped to sell them all.

Quality control was also a problem. Most of the lines had bad reputations. Only Cadillac and Buick were known for quality. Even worse, General Motors

Pierre S. DuPont served as president of General Motors from 1920 to 1923.

had no inventory control. No one knew how many car parts were available for production.

Despite the confusion, Sloan remained optimistic. He realized that General Motors had a major advantage over its main rival, the Ford Motor Company. While Ford had only one car design—the Model T—General Motors had a variety of cars in a variety of price ranges. The automaker that had the most variety would stand to gain the most.

Sloan decided to reorganize GM's line of cars. Most of the cars had four- or six-cylinder engines and fell into

Typical early factory scenes at General Motors show workers dropping an engine into place (above) and putting the final touches on a line of 1918 Chevrolets.

the $1,300 to $1,500 price range. Sloan determined that GM should compete in every price bracket except the very highest. The more expensive the car, the more cylinders it would have.

After reorganizing, this is how the GM lineup looked:

- Chevrolet: 4 cylinders; $525-825
- Oldsmobile: 6 cylinders; $890-1375
- Oakland: 6 cylinders; $1095-1645
- Buick
    Standard: 6 cylinders; $1159-1665
    Master: 6 cylinders; $1395-2425
- Cadillac: 8 cylinders; $3045-4650

Sloan decided that a new model, Pontiac, would fill the gap between Chevrolet and Oldsmobile while the La Salle would fill the gap between Buick and Cadillac.

Once reorganized, Sloan turned his attention to the day-to-day business operations. He discontinued all purchasing until inventories ran down and established inventory controls so the company would experience no shortage or oversupply of parts. And he decided to discontinue any car line that did not sell well.

Sloan also formed a policy of annual model changes. He hoped that would make customers so dissatisfied with their current cars that they would buy new ones. He also revamped the dealer network that sold GM cars throughout the country. And he used advertising,

In 1926, General Motors built its first Pontiac, which was
the company's five-millionth car (above). Below is the 1927
La Salle, designed by professional stylist Harley J. Earl.

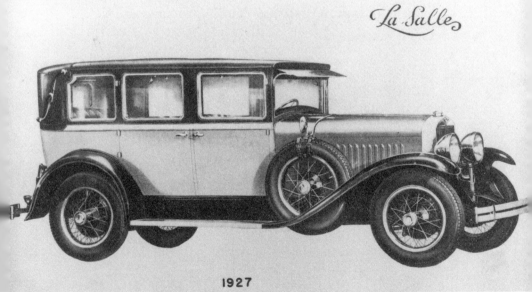

La Salle

1927

searchlights, parades, banquets, and balloons to attract customers and sell cars.

In Sloan's first year at the controls of GM, the company sold 457,000 cars and trucks. Its profits were $61 million. The following year, it sold 800,000 vehicles at an $80-million profit. Pierre DuPont was so pleased that, in 1923, he named Sloan president of GM and promptly retired.

Sloan's masterful guidance of GM continued throughout the decade. In 1929, GM sold 1.9 million cars and trucks and had a profit of $248 million. But the Great Depression, which struck that same year, tested Sloan's business talents to the limit. By 1932, sales had dropped to less than a third of 1929's levels. Still, GM showed a modest profit. And throughout the Depression, the corporation never failed to pay a dividend to its stockholders. Sloan had learned to react quickly to the ever-changing market. Because General Motors was so well organized, change was not difficult.

In 1946, Sloan retired from the presidency but stayed on as chairman of the board until 1956. By then, GM had captured 52 percent of the automobile market. Sloan became a philanthropist, donating much of his fortune to cancer research. The major recipients were the Sloan-Kettering Institute for Cancer Research and the Massachusetts Institute of Technology. By the time he died on February 17, 1966, Sloan had donated a total of $305 million to various organizations.

Above: A 1938 experimental model from General Motors, this "Y-Job" was the first car to feature disappearing headlights. Below; a 1946 Chevrolet, one of the first new models to come out following the end of World War II.

When Alfred P. Sloan, Jr., took charge of General Motors, the company was in turmoil and on the verge of collapse. By looking at the business as well as the product, Sloan was able to reorganize this automaker into one of the greatest success stories of the century.

Enzo Ferrari gave his name to some of the most beloved sports cars in the world.

7

Enzo Ferrari

*O*f all the sports cars in the world, none is more famous than Ferrari.

Enzo Ferrari was born in Modena, Italy, on February 18, 1898. He developed an interest in auto racing at an early age. When Ferrari was ten years old, his father, Alfredo, took him to the car races in Bologna, Italy. There he saw Vincenzo Lancia set a record for the fastest lap. Ferrari was hooked, and he began dreaming of the day when he could drive race cars.

In 1914, when World War I began, the Italian army drafted 16-year-old Ferrari to serve in a mountain artillery unit. During the war, Ferrari's father and brother were killed in action. But Ferrari survived.

After serving in World War I, Ferrari got a job with

Alfa Romeo, a car maker in Turin, Italy. There he worked as a mechanic, a test driver, and a racing driver.

In 1919, Ferrari entered his first race and finished fourth in the *Parma-Berceto*. In 1920, Ferrari drove an Alfa Romeo Grand Prix racing car in the *Targa Florio*. He won second place overall and first in his category. In 1924, Ferrari also won the *Coppa Acerbo* race, and the Italian government named him "Cavaliere." This was an honor because "Cavaliere" was the equivalent of English knighthood.

Enzo Ferrari drove an Alfa Romeo to second place in the 1920 Targa Florio *race.*

Ferrari had become one of Italy's most respected race car drivers. To reward him, Alfa Romeo decided to let Ferrari form *Scuderia Ferrari* (Team Ferrari), the company's racing division.

Ferrari moved his shop into a large, ornate building on the outskirts of Modena. The ground floor housed the workshops. Ferrari and his young family—including his wife, Laura, and son, Dino—lived above. From the side of the building hung a huge banner that proudly displayed Ferrari's name.

Ferrari immediately began building race cars for Alfa Romeo. The 6C 1750, the P2, the Tipo B P3, and the 6C 2300 rolled from the shop. By 1932, Scuderia Ferrari dominated the Grand Prix racing scene across Italy and Europe.

By the late 1930s, German manufacturers—especially Mercedes-Benz—were chipping away at Ferrari's racing success. In 1938, Alfa Romeo began running Scuderia Ferrari from their Milan offices. The company named Ferrari as manager.

Ferrari was a proud and rebellious man. He did not like losing control of his racing shop. After many disputes with Alfa Romeo's chief engineer, Ferrari decided to leave the company in 1939. He returned to Modena and set up Auto Avio Costruzioni, a manufacturing and design firm. There, with the help of 40 employees, Ferrari produced machine tools and oil-driven grinding machines for the auto industry.

*Ferrari, standing at far left, with fellow members of the
1923 Alfa Romeo racing team and their cars*

But just when Ferrari's business began thriving,
Italy's leader, Benito Mussolini, declared war against the
Allies in 1940. Construction of automobiles halted.
The Italian government called upon Ferrari to build war
materials and grinding machines for Italy's war effort.

In 1943, Ferrari moved his shop to Maranello
because Mussolini wanted Italy's factories spread out
across the country to make finding them difficult for the
Allied bombers. Despite the move, the Allies bombed

Benito Mussolini, Italy's leader in World War II, used Ferrari's automotive skills for military purposes.

Ferrari's factory on November 4, 1944, and again in February 1945.

The destruction was great. The bombs leveled much of the brick and timber building. Production did not return to normal until after the war ended in 1945.

As Italy struggled to rebuild, the demand for machine tools grew. While his business boomed, Ferrari worked on race car designs. By 1946, automobile racing had resumed in earnest throughout Italy.

Eager to join in the fun, Ferrari began building his first race car in 1946. Called the Tipo 125, it had a revolutionary V-12 engine. On May 11, 1946, Ferrari entered the car in a race at Piacenza. With two laps to go, the 125 was in the lead. But then a fuel pump failed and forced the car from the race. Despite the setback, Ferrari was pleased with the car's performance. His company built and sold three 125s in 1947. Ferrari was on his way to gaining respect in the racing world.

In 1948, Ferrari introduced the Tipo 166. It, too, had a powerful V-12 with a top speed of 120 MPH. The car won the *Mille Miglia* (1,000 mile) race, which at the time was Italy's most famous and important race. The 166 also won the Paris 12-hour race.

Ferrari's Tipo 166

In 1949, Ferrari's 166 won its first Formula One race, the Grand Prix of Rosario. But the best came later that year. The 166 won Europe's most famous race—the Le Mans 24-hour competition.

Ferrari's success won him widespread acclaim across the international scene. His cars were suddenly in great demand. Orders came in from as far away as the United States.

But there was a problem. Ferraris were still being built by hand in Ferrari's workshops. To increase production, Ferrari expanded the factory and separated race car manufacturing from road car production. And he made sure that his work force was highly specialized, well trained, and equipped with machine tools of top quality. But the company used no production line, and the employees still built the cars by hand.

Ferrari insisted on using top-quality parts to construct his automobiles. When he could, he constructed these parts within the walls of his own factory. His foundry cast engine blocks from aluminum and magnesium alloys. He also had a heat-treating plant that covered parts with shiny chrome.

But a car is made up of hundreds of parts, and Ferrari did not have the machinery, the employees, or the money to build everything for his cars. So, like all other auto makers, Ferrari bought parts from outside suppliers. However, he accepted only the finest parts available.

Skilled craftsmen use precision tools to make Ferrari car parts.

In 1949, his company built 21 cars. Production numbers grew steadily through the early 1950s. In 1953, Ferrari produced 57 cars, just over one per week. By 1956, Ferrari had built a total of 389 automobiles.

The workers worked slowly and carefully. When automobile production started in 1946, Ferrari had 140 employees. By 1955, Ferrari employed 250 workers. Quality, not quantity, remained important to Ferrari. He wanted his workers to take their time when assembling cars. Mass production was not his goal.

In 1952, Ferrari decided his cars needed to look more consistent with each other. He wanted people to take one look at his car and say, "That's a Ferrari!" To do this, Ferrari decided to use one auto body design company. That company was Pininfarina (pin-in-fa-REE-nah). Since 1953, almost all Ferrari body designs have come from this company.

In 1954, Ferrari produced a car that made him and his company a legend: the 250. The most famous 250s were the Testa Rossa and the GT Spyder.

In Italian, *Testa Rossa* means "red head." The name came from a Ferrari mechanic who painted the tops of the 250's engines with red paint. He did this so the 250 engines would not get mixed up with the other Ferrari engines.

The Ferrari 250 had a top speed of 176 MPH and could go from 0 to 100 MPH in 14.1 seconds. Demand for the car became so great that Ferrari had to produce

The Ferrari Testa Rossa

it on his first assembly line. He also began selling the 250 in a car dealer network with foreign importers. Before that, buyers had to purchase a Ferrari directly from the factory.

The 250 remained popular until 1964. By then, Ferrari was making 650 cars per year. Ferrari was in its glory years—sales were never better.

About this time, Enzo Ferrari decided to test the value of his company on the open market. He approached Ford Motor Company of America and offered to sell his company to them. In return, Ferrari wanted $18 million. Negotiations continued for a while, but eventually the deal fell through.

In 1967, Ferrari introduced the Dino series. He named the Dino after his son who had died in June 1956 of kidney failure. The Dino had a V-6 engine instead of the usual Ferrari V-12. It also had a top speed of 146 MPH. But the Dino was incredibly light and agile and could go from 0 to 100 mph in only 9 seconds. The company built 4,000, and the car remained in production for eight years.

At the Paris Auto Show in October 1968, Ferrari introduced the Daytona. At that time, it was the most expensive—$20,000—and fastest road car Ferrari had ever made. The Daytona had a top speed of 174 MPH and went from 0 to 100 MPH in 18.3 seconds. Auto

The Ferrari Dino

The Ferrari Daytona

experts widely called it one of the finest cars ever produced. It quickly became one of Ferrari's all-time best sellers.

In 1969, Enzo Ferrari finally found another auto maker willing to invest in his company. Fiat bought 40 percent of Ferrari, ensuring a long and prosperous future for the company. Now Ferrari could concentrate on building better and faster sports cars without worrying about costs.

Ferrari continued to evolve in the early 1970s. In 1971, the Berlinetta Boxer brought dramatic changes to the Ferrari line of cars. The Berlinetta engine was a "boxer." That is, it had two banks of six cylinders that "punched" at each other from opposite sides. It also had 30 more horsepower than the same size V-12. Moreover, Ferrari placed the engine in the rear—and set the standard for future Ferraris.

What made the car a success was its body design. The Berlinetta was low—3.7 feet—and wide—5.9 feet. Nothing on the road at the time looked like it. The car had a top speed of 188 MPH and could go from 0 to 100 MPH in only 10 seconds. The Berlinetta remained in production until 1984.

The Ferrari Berlinetta Boxer

In 1980, Ferrari introduced its first four-seat convertible: the Mondial. It was the closest thing Ferrari has to a family car. With a top speed of "only" 158 MPH, it was also the slowest. But the Mondial has remained a top seller—outselling many of the more famous sports cars. As of 1993, it was still in production.

In 1984, Ferrari introduced the Testarossa at the Paris Auto Show. Ferrari designed the car with the American market in mind. The Testarossa was the first Ferrari to conform to U.S. safety and emissions standards.

The Testarossa remains Ferrari's only 12-cylinder

The Testarossa, Ferrari's newer version of the Testa Rossa

car in production. It has a top speed of 181 MPH and can go from 0 to 100 MPH in 11.2 seconds. With a 77.8-inch width and 44.5-inch height, the Testarossa is one of the world's widest and lowest cars. But its most memorable feature is the "cheese slicer" air vents on each side.

The next major change in the Ferrari line was the 328 GTB. Powered by a V-8 engine, this 1986 car had a top speed of 156 MPH and cost $64,393. The television show "Magnum P.I." made the 328 GTB famous. The show's star, Tom Selleck, drove a 328 in every episode.

The 328 became Ferrari's best-selling car for the

The 328 GTB

1980s. The company made 5,400 of them but then discontinued production in 1989, making way for the 348—Ferrari's car of the 1990s. Introduced in 1990, after Enzo Ferrari's death, this two-seater boasted a V-8 engine, a top speed of 172 MPH, and the power to go from 0-60 in 5.6 seconds.

On July 21, 1987, 89-year-old Enzo Ferrari was on hand for his company's 40th anniversary in Maranello. At the ceremony, Ferrari stood at the central position of the speaker's table and spoke through his English interpreter.

"Little more than a year ago," he said, "I expressed my wish to the engineers. Build a car to be the best in the world. And now the car is here."

Nearby, a red covering was removed from a car, revealing the new red Ferrari. The engineers had not disappointed their founder. They had designed the ultimate Ferrari—the F40.

The F40 was unlike any Ferrari before it. Its body was made of composite materials (metals, ceramics, and glass), and it had a clear plastic cover over the rear engine—the designers were proud of the powerful V-8 engine and wanted to show it off! The F40 had a top speed of 201 MPH, and could go from 0 to 60 MPH in an incredible 3.5 seconds. It was the first production sports car to surpass the lofty 200 MPH mark. Today, it remains a leader in the world of high-performance cars.

Enzo Ferrari, unfortunately, did not live to see the

*The Ferrari F40—perhaps the most spectacular sports car
ever made*

success of the F40 or the 348. He died on August 14,
1988, and was buried in a private ceremony the next
day. But his contributions to the world of sports car
design have been legendary. Ferrari automobiles
remain one of the most recognized and admired sports
cars on the road today. And their standards for quality
remain unsurpassed.

*Honda Motor Company founder Soichiro Honda stands
proudly beside one of his most successful products, the Accord.*

8
Soichiro Honda

*I*f ever a name changed the way we think about the automotive industry, it is Honda. In a short time, Honda Motor Company has become one of the world's largest automobile manufacturers. Its founder, Soichiro Honda, has been hailed by many as one of the last great businessmen. He forged a motorcycle and automobile empire from mechanical intuition and from sheer tenacity—eventually building the best-selling car in the United States.

Soichiro Honda was born on November 17, 1906, in Hamamatsu, Japan, about 150 miles southwest of Tokyo. The son of a blacksmith, Honda's earliest experiences around his father's smoky shop developed his fascination with machinery. When Honda was eight years old, he saw a motorcar for the first time. The machine dumbfounded Honda. He vowed that one day he would build his own car.

Although he was bright, Honda was not a good student. He was a doer, not a thinker. When he was 15 years old, Honda left school to become an apprentice at Art Shokai, a car repair shop in Tokyo. But the job was a major disappointment because the shop had squads of mechanics. Honda's chief responsibility was baby-sitting the boss's children.

Honda's big break came at the misfortune of many. In 1923, Tokyo suffered the Great Kanto earthquake. In the aftermath, most of the shop's employees fled Tokyo. Only Honda and a senior apprentice remained. Thus, Honda received all the technical training and experience he had hoped for.

In 1928, Honda returned to Hamamatsu to set up a branch of the Art Shokai repair shop. In his spare time, Honda tinkered with race car designs because he secretly yearned to become a race car driver.

In 1936, Honda won his first racing trophy at the All-Japan Speed Rally. There he set a record speed of 75 MPH. But Honda never crossed the finish line. His car crashed, nearly killing him. After a slow recovery, Honda decided that his race car driving days were over. Instead, he would concentrate his efforts on building better engines.

Honda started Tokai Seike Heavy Industry Company, to build piston rings. To learn more about metal-working, Honda attended a local technical high school. Honda's experiences at the school were bittersweet. While he learned valuable information, he was not suited to the classroom. Honda, an intelligent student, was impatient with textbook studying and examinations. So the school refused to give him a diploma.

Although he lacked formal training, Honda possessed remarkable mechanical intuition. He seemed to know how to solve a mechanical problem without examining the situation. When others questioned Honda's intuition, he would first become stubborn. Then he would relent and try other methods. In the end, Honda's intuition was usually correct.

When World War II began, Honda's piston company supplied tools for aircraft propellers. But Allied bombing raids nearly destroyed the factory. Distraught, Honda sold what was left to the Toyota Motor Company and took a year off. He stayed at home, relaxing and making homemade whiskey. He also worked on a design for a rotary weaving machine and a commercial application to extract salt from seawater.

But Honda's concern for his country soon brought him back into the world of manufacturing. Japan was still in ruins from the war, and the country desperately needed transportation vehicles. Because of this, Honda had uncovered a tremendous business opportunity.

The military had a surplus of 500 small generator engines. Honda bought the engines at a bargain price and attached them to bicycle frames. Before long, Honda was making his own small engines. Each was capable of running on pine-resin fuel. In a time when gasoline was hard to find, these engines proved invaluable to the Japanese people. With the success of his engines, Honda was able to manufacture his own bicycle frames.

In September 1948, with only $1,500, Honda formed the Honda Motor Company in Hamamatsu. There he began building a full line of powerful and well-engineered motorcycles. The legend of Honda had begun.

Honda motorcycles sold well throughout Japan. But because good motorcycle parts were still difficult to obtain, Honda workers had to file down faulty parts to make them work. Still, Honda insisted that the parts be perfect. He loudly scolded any worker who did not do the job properly. Sloppiness, he often pointed out, could cost people their lives. His short temper earned him the nickname "Mr. Thunder." But he was also a patient man and would often help workers who encountered technical difficulties. To Honda, quality—not quantity—was important.

In March 1950, Honda established a sales branch in Tokyo. By September, Honda had built a Tokyo factory. To keep up with the growing demand, plant expansion continued at a rapid pace during the next few years. In 1952, the Shirako factory was completed. In 1953, the

Honda's first motorcycle, the 1949 Dream

Yamato plant was producing Honda motorcycles. Honda Motor Company had become so large that it began trading company stock on the Tokyo Stock Exchange.

In 1954, Honda invested a substantial sum of money in machine tools. But then a recession hit Japan hard and creditors nearly shut the company down. Still, Honda emerged quickly from the recession. By 1955, Honda Motor Company took the lead in Japan's motorcycle production. By 1958, Honda became the first company in the world to sell more than one million motorcycles in a year.

Slowly, Honda began to export its motorcycles to America. Sales were slow at first because Americans thought that Japanese products were second rate. But once the American public recognized the quality and performance of Honda motorcycles, sales took off. By 1959, Honda motorcycles became an international success story, establishing American Honda Motor Company in the United States. This international expansion was followed, in 1961, by the establishment of Honda Deutschland in Hamburg, West Germany. By the early 1960s, Honda was the world's largest manufacturer of motorcycles and sales topped 100,000 units a month—something that had never been done before.

From this international success, Honda decided to enter the automobile market in 1962. But Honda's dream was not well received by his country's government. Japan's powerful Ministry of International Trade and Industry did not want Honda to build automobiles. Japan already had two major car manufacturers—Toyota and Nissan. The government feared that too many Japanese cars on the market might hurt the economy.

Honda ignored the government's cool response to his plans. His first vehicle was the S-360, a mini-sized sports car with a small, whiny engine. Again, foreign markets considered the Japanese product a joke and did not take it seriously.

During the 1960s, Honda's great reputation as a manufacturer of high-quality motorcycles hurt its entry into the automobile market. People viewed Honda motorcycles as products for fun and recreation. Buying a car was a more serious purchase. Introduced to the United States in 1969, the N-600 did little to change this attitude. The N-600, with its small, high-revving engine and miniaturized body, was dwarfed by its larger, more substantial competitors. As a result, many customers thought of it as just another Honda motorcycle disguised as an automobile.

But sales of Honda cars grew slowly but steadily from the late 1960s into the early 1970s. Then in July

The Honda N-600, first exported to the United States in 1969

1972, Honda introduced the Civic 1200. It represented Honda's first serious contender in the international automobile market. The Civic appeared just when the world was experiencing an oil crisis. Because the car had low fuel consumption, it became an instant success.

In 1977, the Honda Civic ranked first in the Fuel Economy Test for 1977 models. The test was conducted by America's Environmental Protection Agency (EPA). The ranking added to the Civic's growing acceptance and popularity.

Before this happened, however, Soichiro Honda retired and became one of the company's supreme advisors in October 1973. But Honda made a point not to interfere with the management of the company he founded and he let the managers run the company. Somehow, Honda knew that his way of doing things did not work in such a large company.

Throughout his long career, Honda never played the role of a traditional businessman. He spent most of his time in the research lab—and away from the board room. Honda left most of the administrative work to his partner, Takeo Fujisawa. Honda never brought work home with him and he drew a clear line between the job and off hours. Even at work, he promptly broke for lunch.

Honda introduced its most successful automobile in 1976. It was a small passenger car called the Accord. In 1978, Honda increased its presence in the automobile

Budget-minded car buyers turned to Honda's 1973 Civic to get better gas mileage.

market when it introduced the Prelude. In 1980, Honda announced that it would build a car manufacturing plant in Ohio. Thus, Honda became the first Japanese auto maker to build cars in the United States. "I found doing business here much easier than in Japan," Soichiro Honda said. "Our company in Ohio has been so well accepted that I believe it is an American company in substance."

In October 1989, American auto executives invited Soichiro Honda to Detroit, Michigan, for a very special honor. Before an audience of 800 auto-industry elite,

A fine example of Honda styling, the 1993 Civic del Sol

Honda became the first Japanese auto maker to be inducted into the Automotive Hall of Fame, joining the likes of Henry Ford. At the time, Honda's company had put 1.4 million American-made Hondas on the road. Since 1970, Honda had sold 5.1 million imports.

Soichiro Honda died in August 5, 1991, of liver failure. Following his wishes, no company funeral was held. Honda was cremated in a private gathering that was attended by 40 relatives and friends.

The life of Soichiro Honda was more than a rags-to-riches story. Like the biblical David, Honda took on such Goliaths as General Motors and Ford and defeated them on their own turf. His world-class cars set new auto standards and transformed an entire industry. Sadly, Honda's death marked the end of an era—a time when an individual could still create an empire out of nothing more than sheer determination.

Had Ferruccio Lamborghini not left his family farm, car lovers throughout the world would never haved enjoyed his special automotive design talents.

142

9

Ferruccio Lamborghini

*T*he Lamborghini is not a common sight on the highway. But when you see one, you never forget it. Since the company was founded in 1963, it has built some of the fastest and most unusual sports cars the world has ever known.

Ferruccio (fair-ROOCH-ee-oh) Lamborghini was born on April 28, 1916, in Renazzo di Cento, a small village 15 miles north of Bologna, Italy. The Lamborghini family were peasant farmers, and Lamborghini spent his early years in the fields of the family farm. Working with crude farm equipment sparked an interest in mechanics.

Young Lamborghini often expressed his dislike for farming, so his family enrolled him at an industrial college near Bologna. He graduated just before World

War II broke out in Europe. During the war, Lamborghini served with the mechanical detachment of the Italian Air Force. There, his interest in and knowledge of engineering grew. He constantly worked on cars, motorcycles, tractors, and airplanes. Working with the shortages and pressures of wartime conditions taught him to improvise.

After World War II ended, Lamborghini returned to the family farm. But the war had devastated the Italian countryside, leaving a critical shortage of farm machinery. Remembering his improvisation lessons, Lamborghini gathered leftover war vehicles, including tanks, and built homemade tractors. Soon he built a factory near Bologna where he manufactured diesel tractors. By the mid-1950s, his Lamborghini Tractor Company had become one of Italy's largest farm equipment manufacturers.

By now, Lamborghini was a millionaire. But he was not content just to manufacture tractors. He had his eye on the automobile industry and had a secret ambition to design the ultimate Grand Touring automobile—something that was better than anything yet manufactured.

In 1963, Lamborghini bought land in St. Agata, a small village between Bologna and Modena. There he built an ultramodern factory and equipped it with the best machinery. Then he hired Giotti Bizzarrini, who had worked for Italian auto maker Alfa Romeo, to be his engine designer. Lamborghini was now ready to build the ultimate driving machine.

Lamborghini's first automobile was the two-seat 350 GT with a V-12 engine and a top speed of 150 MPH. From 1964-1966, Lamborghini built 120 of these large but graceful cars.

The 400 GT quickly followed. It looked similar to the 350 GT, but its engine was larger and more powerful. The company built 23 in 1966 before the 400 GT 2+2 appeared. Lamborghini's company manufactured 250 of them before production of the 400 series finally ended in 1968. Many auto experts and sports car lovers

Having successfully built tractors, Ferruccio Lamborghini turned his attention to making flashy vehicles, such as the 350 GT.

consider the 400 series to be the best Lamborghinis ever built.

Lamborghini was pleased with his first automobiles, but they still did not represent the ultimate driving machine he had dreamed about. Nor were they huge commercial successes.

The Miura (Me-YOUR-ah) changed all that. Introduced in 1966 at the Geneva Auto Show, the Miura created an international sensation. Named after a Spanish fighting bull, the Miura's design was revolutionary. It had low, sleek lines; the latest technology; and a top speed of 170 MPH—by far the fastest road car of its day. Overnight, Lamborghini became the new leader of exotic sports cars.

Lamborghini built 764 Miuras. But the revolutionary design proved difficult to maintain. Even worse, the car was hot, noisy, and uncomfortable. Although the Miura had made Lamborghini a world-class sports car manufacturer, production ended in 1972.

While he had still been producing the Miura, Lamborghini corrected its flaws and came up with the Espada (es-PAH-da). Introduced in 1968, the Espada became Lamborghini's most popular car of the 1960s and 1970s.

Big and roomy, the Espada could seat four passengers comfortably. With its powerful V-12 engine and a top speed of 155 MPH, it was the fastest four-seater on the road. Because the car was so versatile, 1,220

Introduced in 1966, the Miura represented Lamborghini's first big breakthrough in the sports car market.

Espadas were built. It remained in production until 1978.

Lamborghini also introduced another car in 1968: the Islero (eez-LAIR-oh), which replaced the 400 GT. The Islero with its covered headlights, V-12 engine, and a top speed of 160 MPH, could go from 0 to 60 MPH in 6.2 seconds.

Ferruccio Lamborghini had a major role in the Islero's design. He wanted a big, roomy, and fast "businessman's car." However, although the Islero was well constructed, it could not compete with the revolutionary Miura and the ever popular Espada. The company built only 225 and ceased production in April 1970.

By 1972, Ferruccio Lamborghini grew tired of his auto company's financial problems. Workers were often

The Islero

on strike, and his cars had difficulty in passing the tough American safety and emission control laws that restricted the amount of a car's exhaust. He sold 51 percent of his company to Swiss businessman George-Henri Rosetti and lost control of day-to-day operations—including auto design.

But the Lamborghini company did not cease operations. That same year, it introduced the Urraco (you-RAH-koe)—the first Lamborghini to use a V-8 engine. However, its back seat was too small to hold passengers. Overall, the car was disappointing, and the company discontinued it in 1979 after building only 780.

In 1974, Ferruccio Lamborghini sold the remaining 49 percent of his company to another Swiss business-man, Rene Leimer. Ferruccio Lamborghini was now officially out of the auto making business. He returned to the family farm in Panicarola, where he grew grapes in retirement.

The two Swiss businessman kept the name Lamborghini for their company as they struggled to make it profitable. In 1976, the company introduced the two-seat Silhouette. It, too, had a V-8 engine. It was also the first Lamborghini to offer a removable top. But because the Silhouette looked too much like the Urraco, sales were poor. The company built only 52 and ended production in 1979.

In 1978, the Lamborghini automobile company declared bankruptcy. This move prevented the auto maker from going out of business. The Swiss owners sold the company to the Mimran family, who invested the money necessary to keep production going. The family maintained the legendary name of Lamborghini.

After reorganizing, the Lamborghini company introduced the Jalpa in 1982. The Jalpa was the company's final attempt at a V-8 automobile. But Lamborghini buyers wanted the bigger, more powerful V-12 engine. Sales remained slow, and the company discontinued the Jalpa in 1988 after producing 410.

The company founded by Lamborghini seemed destined to fail. But the Countach saved it. The company introduced the Countach in 1971 at the Geneva Auto Show. There it was hailed as a major breakthrough in automotive design. Besides its sleek, aerodynamic lines and V-12 engine, the Countach's most notable feature was its doors that swung up to open. Another trademark was its pop-up headlights. Despite all the praise, the Countach wasn't the perfect automobile. Because of its poor rear visibility, the driver had to open the door, sit on the door sill, and peer above the roof line in order to back up.

The Countach had five different models during its 18-year reign as the most acclaimed sports car of its time. But Lamborghini didn't realize the Countach's true value until the 1980s when the company experienced its most trying times.

In 1982, the company introduced the Countach LP500 with its top speed of 185 MPH. Lamborghini produced a total of 323 before replacing it with the Countach Quattrovalvole in 1985. With the success of the Countach, Lamborghini emerged from its financial woes. Suddenly, its future looked much brighter.

Lamborghini's rebound caught the attention of the Chrysler Corporation of America. Chrysler bought the Lamborghini company in 1987 and decided to remain with the company's strength—the Countach.

In 1988, Chrysler built the fifth and final Countach and called it the "25th Anniversary" in recognition of Lamborghini's founding in 1963. The most distinctive feature of the 25th Anniversary was the air scoops in front of the wheels. The 25th Anniversary, the most popular Countach ever, had a top speed of 184 MPH and could go from 0 to 60 mph in only 5 seconds.

From 1988 to 1990, Chrysler built 650 of the popular 25th Anniversary Countachs. In all, 1,972

*Above: Lamborghini's first Countach, on display at the 1971
Geneva Auto Show. Below: the 25th Anniversary
Countach—a fitting symbol of Ferruccio's quarter century in
the sports car business*

Countachs were produced—earning Lamborghini its legendary status in the world of exotic sports cars.

With the 25th Anniversary Countach, Lamborghini was at its best. No one dreamed the company could come up with something better—but that's exactly what Lamborghini did.

In 1990, Lamborghini introduced the Diablo, which looks like the Countach, only sleeker. With its traditional V-12 engine, it had a top speed of 202 MPH and went from 0 to 60 mph in a mere 4 seconds. That made the Diablo the world's fastest road car.

Even more remarkable was the Diablo's biggest innovation: four-wheel drive—all four wheels, not just the usual front or rear wheels, propelled the car. Lamborghini had done it! It had produced an all-wheel drive car that could travel over 200 MPH!

The Diablo was the best aerodynamically designed Lamborghini to date. Its low, sleek lines allowed the Diablo to slice through the air with minimal resistance—a vast improvement over the Countach.

The company made other major improvements to the doors and windows. The doors still opened upward, but they had a lower sill for easier passenger entry. The windows opened downward into the doors, and the dip toward the front wheel offered greater side visibility.

The Countach enjoyed great success for 18 years. Enthusiasts hailed it as the sports car of the 1970s and 1980s. With the introduction of the Diablo,

Lamborghini has claimed the sports car of the 1990s. Its exotic design will undoubtedly keep the Diablo on top into the next century.

When Ferruccio Lamborghini started the company that still bears his name, he wanted to build the ultimate sports car. After a few attempts, Lamborghini set the standard with the Miura. The Lamborghini legend had begun.

Ferruccio Lamborghini died on February 20, 1993, and even though he had been out of the world of exotic automobile design since 1974, the company has remained true to its founder. For the Diablo—the future of the Lamborghini automobile company—owed its design and existence to the Countach, introduced while Lamborghini was still part of the company, and to Ferruccio Lamborghini's vision.

Lamborghini's car of the 1990s—the four-wheel drive Diablo

Bibliography

Boesen, Victor. *The Mercedes-Benz Book.* New York: Doubleday, 1981.

Clark, Paul. *Lamborghini Countach.* London: Osprey Publishing, 1988.

Clausager, Anders Ditlev. *Porsche.* New York: St. Martin's Press, 1983.

Dregni, Michael. *Inside Ferrari.* Osceola, WI: Motorbooks International, 1990.

Jellinek-Mercedes, Guy. *My Father, Mr. Mercedes.* Radnor, PA: Chilton, 1961.

Lathan, Caroline. *Dodge Dynasty: The Car & the Family that Rocked Detroit.* San Diego: Harcourt Brace Jovanovich, 1989.

Lozier, Herbert. *Car of Kings.* Radnor, PA: Chilton, 1967.

Porter, Philip. *Jaguar: History of a Classic Marque.* New York: Orion Books, 1988.

Sakiya, Tetsuo. *Honda Motor: The Men, the Management, the Machines.* New York: Kodansha International, 1982.

Shook, Robert L. *Honda: An American Success Story.* New York: Prentice Hall Press, 1988.

Sloan, Alfred Pritchard. *My Years with General Motors.* New York: Anchor Books, 1972.

Weitman, Julius. *Porsche Story.* New York: Arco Publishing, 1985.

Wherry, Joseph H. *Jaguar Story.* Radnor, PA: Chilton, 1967.

Yates, Brock. *Enzo Ferrari: The Man, the Cars, the Races, the Machine.* New York: Doubleday, 1991.

Index

Accord, Honda, 130, 138
Alfa Romeo, 70-71, 114-115,
  116, 144
All-Japan Speed Rally, 132
Art Shokai, 132
assembly line, 9, 35-36, 37, 46
Austin-Swallow, 85
Autoar, 78
Auto Avio Costruzione, 115
Automotive Hall of Fame, 140
Avery, Clarence, 36

ball bearings, 100-101
Benz, Berta (Mrs. Karl Benz),
  12
Benz, Karl, 8, 10; and car rac-
  ing, 14, 20; company estab-
  lished by, 12, 13, 17, 21;
  death of, 22; early years of,
  11-12; first cars designed by,
  12-14, 16; merger of, with
  Daimler, 21, 22
Benz & Co. 12, 17, 21; merger
  of, with Daimler, 21, 22
Benz cars: Blitzen, 20; Grand
  Prix, 20; Phaeton, 14, 15;
  Victoria, 13
Bizzarrini, Giotti, 144
British Leyland, 93, 94, 95, 96
British Motor Corporation
  (B.M.C.), 93

British Motor Holdings
  (B.M.H.), 93, 94
Bryant, Clara (Mrs. Henry
  Ford), 30, 31, 44, 46
Buick, 104, 107

Cadillac, 104, 107
Chevrolet, 104, 106, 107, 110
Chrysler Corporation, 150
Cistitalia, 78
Civic, Honda, 138, 139, 140
Countach (Lamborghini) 149-
  153
Crossley Motors, 83

Daimler, Gottlieb, 11; death of,
  18; early years of, 14-15;
  engines built by, 14-15, 16-
  17; first cars of, 15-16, 17;
  and Mercedes, 18-20, 26
Daimler-Benz, 71, 72, 76
Daimler company, 16, 18, 70,
  72, 76; Austrian, 68, 69, 70
Daimler Motoren Gesellschaft
  (DMG), 18; merger of, with
  Benz, 21, 22
Daytona Beach, 19, 20
Detroit Automobile Company,
  32-33
Diablo (Lamborghini), 152-153
Diesel, Rudolf, 21

diesel engine, 21
Dodge, Daniel (father), 50, 51
Dodge, John Francis, 48, 49-50,
    53, 55, 56, 57-58; death of,
    58. *See also* Dodge brothers.
Dodge, Horace Elgin, 48, 49-
    50, 51, 53, 55, 56, 57, 59;
    death of, 58. *See also* Dodge
    brothers.
Dodge brothers: and bicycle
    business, 51, 52, companies
    established by, 51, 53, 55;
    early years of, 49-50; first car
    of, 55-56; success of, 53, 55-
    56, 57-59; work of, for Ford,
    33, 49, 53-55; work of, for
    Oldsmobile, 52-53
Dodge Brothers (company), 51,
    53, 55
Dodge Brothers Motor Car
    Company, 56-57
DuPont, Pierre, 103, 104, 105,
    109
Durant, William, 102-103

Earl, Harley, 108
Edison Illuminating Company,
    31, 32
electric car, 63-67
Elizabeth II (queen of England),
    91, 93
Evans, Fred S., 51
Evans & Dodge Bicycle
    Company, 51

Fair Lane, 37, 38, 46
Ferdinand (tank), 76
Ferrari, Alfredo (father), 113
Ferrari, Dino(son), 115, 123
Ferrari, Enzo, death of, 128,
    129; as designer of race cars,
    117-119; early years of, 113;
    and Fiat, 124; production
    methods of, 119, 120, 121; as
    race car driver, 114-115, 116;

sports cars produced by, 90,
    112, 118-128; work of, for
    Alfa Romeo, 114, 115; dur-
    ing WWII, 116-117
Ferrari, Laura (Mrs. Enzo
    Ferrari), 115
Ferrari cars: Berlinetta Boxer,
    124, 125; Daytona, 123-124;
    Dino series, 123; F40, 128-
    129; GT Spyder, 121;
    Mondial, 126; Testa Rossa,
    121, 122, 126; Testarossa,
    126-127; Tipo 166, 118;
    Tipo 125, 118; 348, 128, 129;
    328 GTB, 127-128; 250s,
    121-122
F40 (Ferrari), 128-129
Fiat, 124
Ford, Edsel, 36, 45, 46
Ford, Henry, 7, 8, 75-76, 140;
    company established by, 28,
    33-36, 39, 42, 44-47; death
    of, 46-47; and Dodge broth-
    ers, 33, 49, 53-55; early years
    of, 29-30; first car developed
    by, 31-33; and Model A, 33,
    34, 36, 40-41; and Model T,
    29, 34-35, 36, 38, 39-40, 54;
    production methods of, 9,
    34, 35-36; and unions, 44
Ford, Henry II, 45, 47
Ford Manufacturing Company,
    54
Ford Motor Company, 57, 101,
    102, 105, 122, 140; assembly
    line used by, 35-36, 37; and
    Dodge Brothers, 33, 49, 53-
    55; early years of, 33-35;
    founding of, 33; during
    Great Depression, 42; and
    Jaguar, 96; and Model A, 33,
    34, 36, 40-41; and Model T,
    34-35, 38, 39-40, 54, 102,
    105; unionization of, 44; and
    V-8, 42, 43; during WWI,

156

37-39; during WWII, 45
four-wheel drive, 152
front-wheel drive, 9, 64, 67, 81
Fujisawa, Takeo, 138

gasoline-powered engine, 12,
    14, 15; developed by Ford,
    30-32; water-cooled, 15
General Motors (GM), 98, 99,
    140; cars produced by, 104,
    105, 106, 107, 108, 110; early
    years of, 102, 103; problems
    of, 104-105; and purchase of
    Hyatt Co., 102; reorganiza-
    tion of, under Sloan, 107,
    109; sales of, 109
General Motors cars: Buick,
    104, 107; Cadillac, 104, 107;
    Chevrolet, 104, 106, 107,
    110; Oldsmobile, 104, 107;
    Pontiac, 107, 108
Grand Prix, 20, 114, 115, 119
Great Depression, 42

Hawkins, Ivy, 50
Hitler, Adolf, 8, 74, 78
Honda, Soichiro: abilities of,
    131, 133, 134, 138; death of,
    140; early years of, 131-132;
    and founding of Honda
    Motor Co., 130, 134; and
    manufacture of motorcycles,
    134-135, 136, 137; retire-
    ment of, 138; during WW II,
    133
Honda cars: Accord, 130, 138;
    Civic, 138, 139, 140; N-600,
    137; Prelude, 139; S-360, 136
Honda Motor Company, 130,
    131; cars made by, 136-139;
    founding of, 134; and manu-
    facture of motorcycles, 134-
    135, 136, 137; plants of, in
    U.S., 139, 140; sales of, in
    U.S., 136, 137, 138, 140

Hyatt, John Wesley, 100
Hyatt Roller Bearing Company,
    100-102

Jaguar cars: C-Type, 90, 92; D-
    Type, 90, 91, 92; Mark VII,
    88-90; SS, 86; SS 100, 86, 87;
    XJ series, 96; XJ6, 94-95, 96;
    XK-E, 92-93; XK series, 88,
    89
Jaguar company, 83; and British
    Leyland, 93, 94, 95, 96; cars
    produced by, 9, 86-87, 88-
    91, 92, 93; founding of, 86;
    merger of, with B.M.C, 93;
    purchased by Ford, 96; race
    cars of, 90-93; during WWII,
    87
Jellinek, Emil, 17-18

Kaes, Aloisia Johanna (Mrs.
    Ferdinand Porsche), 67-68

Lamborghini, Ferruccio: com-
    pany bought by Chrysler,
    150; death of, 153; early years
    of, 8, 142, 143-144; first cars
    of, 145-146; and manufacture
    of tractors, 144; retirement
    of, 148; sports cars of, 146-
    147
Lamborghini cars: Countach,
    149-150, 151; Diablo, 152-
    153; Espada, 146-147; Islero,
    147, 148; Jalpa,149; Miura,
    146, 147, 153; Silhouette,
    149; 350 GT, 145; 400 GT
    series, 145-146, 147; Urraco,
    148, 149
Lamborghini Tractor
    Company, 144
Lancia, Vincenzo, 113
La Salle, 107, 108
Leimer, Rene, 148
Le Mans, 24, 90, 91, 119

Lohner, Jacob, 63-64, 66, 68
Lohner-Porsche Chaise, 64-67
Lyons, William: death of, 95;
    and design of motorcycle
    sidecars, 84-85; early years
    of, 8, 82, 83-84; first cars of,
    85-86; and Jaguar Co., 86-
    92, 96; knighting of, 91; and
    merger with B.M.C, 93

Malcomson, Alexander, 33
Mark VII (Jaguar), 88-90
Maybach, Wilhelm, 15
Mercedes, 18-20, 21, 70-71;
    races of, 19-20
Mercedes-Benz (company), 10,
    21, 22, 23-27, 90, 115
Mercedes-Benz cars: 450 SL,
    26; Mannheim, 21, 22; S-
    Class, 24, 27; 600 SEC, 27;
    Stuttgart, 21, 22; T 80, 23;
    300, 24, 26; 300 SL, 24, 25;
    230 SL, 26; 220, 24;
    Unimog, 23; W125, 22;
    W25, 22
Messerschmitt airplanes, 23
Mille Miglia, 118
Mimran family, 149
Miura, 146, 147, 153
Model A, 33, 34, 36; second,
    40-41
Model T, 29, 34-35, 36, 38, 39-
    40, 54, 102, 105
Monte Carlo races, 90
motorcycles, 15, 72, 74, 82, 83,
    84; Honda, 134-135, 136,
    137
Mouse (tank), 77
Murphy Boiler Works, 50, 51
Mussolini, Benito, 116, 117

Newbury, Truman, 39
Nissan, 136

Oakland, 107

Old Betsy, 56
Oldfield, Barney, 20
Olds, Ransom, 52
Oldsmobile Corporation, 52-53
Oldsmobile (car), 104, 107
Olds Motor Company, 101

Panther (tank), 23
Phoenix, Daimler, 17
Pininfarina, 121
Pontiac, 107, 108
Porsche, Anna (mother), 62
Porsche, Anton (father), 60, 61-
    63
Porsche, cars designed by:
    Austria, 71; 959, 81; Sascha,
    69-70; 356, 79-80;
    Volksauto, 73-74; Volks-
    wagen, 8, 74-75, 78, 79;
    Wanderer, 72
Porsche, Ferdinand, 8, 9, 21,
    23; death of, 80; design com-
    pany established by, 72-73,
    74; early years of, 8, 60, 61-
    63; electric car of, 64-67; and
    Porsche 356, 78, 79-80; in
    Russia, 73-74; and Volks-
    wagen, 8, 74-75, 78, 79;
    work of for Daimler, 68-71,
    72, 76; work of, for Lohner,
    64-66, 68; work of, for Steyr,
    71; during WWII, 76-78
Porsche, Ferry (son), 68, 76, 78,
    79, 81
Porsche, Oskar (brother), 60

Rabe, Karl, 78
racing automobile, 14, 15, 17,
    19, 20, 33, 87, 113, 132; in
    France, 14, 17, 19-20, 24, 90,
    91, 118, 119; in Germany,
    22-23, 66, 67, 74; in Italy,
    70-71, 113, 114-115, 117-
    118. *See also* individual races.
Roger, Emile, 14

Rogers, Will, 46
Rosenberger, Adolf, 72, 74
Rosetti, George-Henri, 148
Scuderia Ferrari (Team Ferrari), 115
Searles, John, 101
self-starter, 39, 40
Selleck, Tom, 127
Semmering Road, 66
Sloan, Alfred P. Jr.: death of, 110; as manager of ball bearing company, 100-102; early years of, 99-100; as executive of GM, 98, 103, 104, 105, 109, 111; as philanthropist, 109-110; reorganization of, at GM, 107, 109
Sorenson, Charles, 36
SS Cars Ltd., 86
Standard-Swallow, 85, 86
Steyr Works, 71
Stokes, Donald Gresham, 93, 94
supercharged engine, 21
Swallow cars: Austin, 85; SS 1, 86; Standard, 85, 86
Swallow Sidecar Company, 84-85

Targa Florio, 70-71, 114
Taylor, Frederick Winslow, 36
Testa Rossa, 121, 122, 126

Testarossa, 126-127
Thompson, Anna, 51
300 SL (Mercedes-Benz), 24-25; accident of, at Le Mans, 24
Tiger (tank), 23, 76
Tokai Seike Heavy Industry Co., 132
Toyota Motor Company, 133, 136

unions, 44
United Auto Workers (UAW), 44
United Motors Corporation, 102
Universal Credit Company, 41

Volksauto, 73-74
Volkswagen, 8, 74-75, 78, 79

Walmsley, William, 84
Wanderer, 72
Wilson, Woodrow, 38
World Exhibition (1900), 64, 66
WW I, 20-21, 37-38, 69, 113
WWII, 23, 44-45, 76, 77, 87, 116, 117, 133, 144

Y-Job, 110

Zundapp Works, 72

Photo Credits

ABOUT THE AUTHOR

ROBERT ITALIA has been an editor and author since 1982. He specializes in biographies, history, and sports, and has written more than 50 children's books. His titles include *Legendary Sports Heroes* (1988), *Snowboarding* (1990), *Mountain Biking* (1990), *War in the Gulf* (1991), *Reaching for the Stars* (1991), and *General H. Norman Schwarzkopf (1992)*. He has also adapted movie and television properties for the school and library market. Italia was born and raised in Chicago. He now lives in Minneapolis, where he continues to write and edit children's books. He drives a Lexus.